Learning and Programmed Instruction

Learning and Programmed Instruction

JULIAN I. TABER, *Western Reserve University*

ROBERT GLASER, *University of Pittsburgh*

HALMUTH H. SCHAEFER, *Patton State Hospital*

 ADDISON-WESLEY READING, MASSACHUSETTS

ADDISON-WESLEY PUBLISHING COMPANY, INC.
READING, MASSACHUSETTS · Palo Alto · London
NEW YORK · DALLAS · ATLANTA · BARRINGTON, ILLINOIS

Preface

While the implications of the science of learning for educational practice are not limited to particular theories or approaches to the study of behavior, it is certainly true that the present interest in programmed instruction and teaching machines is specifically attributable to the writings of Professor B. F. Skinner in 1955 and 1958.* It is Skinner's work which has captured the general imagination, and his transition from laboratory studies to practical application has encouraged a systematic basis for further research and development in teaching. The language and technology of Skinner's laboratory provide the framework for most recently published programmed materials.

Initial developments spring into being with the errors and inefficiencies of first inventions. However, these early developments, if they are at all challenging, provide a basis for continued development and correction and a target for constructive revision. With this in mind, the attempt has been made in this book to discuss the principles that contributed to these first steps in programmed instruction, which have led to present practices, and which can shape their improvement. These early attempts pertained to what can be called verbal, linear, small-step programming, although the general principles involved are not restricted only to verbal behavior or to this type of format, since the properties of both the category of behavior involved and the kind of subject matter being taught can radically influence instructional format. Subsidiary practices, developed away from the mainstream are mentioned in this book, but the attempt has been made to provide a sustained point of view.

---

* Skinner, B. F., "The science of learning and the art of teaching." In *Current trends in psychology and the behavioral sciences,* Pittsburgh: University of Pittsburgh Press, 1955. Skinner, B. F., "Teaching machines." *Science* **128**, 969–977, 1958. Both are reprinted in *Teaching Machines and Programmed Learning* (edited by A. A. Lumsdaine and R. Glaser), Washington, D.C.: National Education Association, 1960.

At the present stage of development of programmed instruction, there is little substitute for research, development, and demonstration. These efforts, however, must take place on the basis of underlying principles and not outward appearances. Most published programmed instructional materials have linear, small-step formats, but this format is based on some underlying knowledge about the learning process. The improperly initiated practitioner may learn only to imitate the format and ignore the principles. It is primarily for this reason that this book discusses principles as well as procedures.

This book grew out of a manual developed for the Air Force under the sponsorship of the Training Research Branch, Behavioral Sciences Laboratory. The manual given to the Air Force profited greatly from the advice and comments of Dr. Felix Kopstein, Dr. Ross Morgan, and Dr. Alvin Ugelow. An early version of the present manuscript received constructive comments from Professors Robert C. Silverman and Susan M. Markle. In the course of writing the present book, detailed editorial and revision efforts were provided by Mrs. Nancy A. Hoisman. Materials and references for Chapters 4 and 8 were compiled by Margaret Fullick; Miss Fullick also edited the final version of the manuscript. Appreciation is due to Mrs. Ruth Ann Vogt for the details of final manuscript preparation.

J.I.T.
R.G.
H.H.S.

January 1965

Contents

CHAPTER ONE

Introductory Overview

Most of the work on programmed instruction seeks to apply knowledge of the learning process. The empirical facts have been known for some time, but only recently have they been quite seriously applied to the development of instructional devices and procedures. This relationship to scientific underpinnings offers the potential for teaching many subject matters much more effectively than they are taught at the present time. In addition, the efficiency of these new techniques can be evaluated more severely and precisely than has been possible with other teaching methods. When the question "Does this textbook or lecture teach effectively?" is asked, it is frequently answered on the authority of the textbook writer, editor, or lecturer. However, when this question is asked of programmed material, it can be answered by a detailed analysis of whether the behavior of the student is up to the standard of achievement established by the programmer.

The success of programmed instruction depends upon the construction and arrangement of the subject matter material. This material must be built in such a way as to present learning tasks and experiences to the student so that he performs activities that contribute to learning objectives. Sometimes machines can facilitate the presentation of material to students and can provide appropriate ways for them to respond. However, whether programmed instructional procedures require machines or are in textbook form, the construction of the programmed instructional sequence is the important concern. It is primarily the development of these instructional sequences and their subsequent use in schools that involve the interaction between the science of learning and teaching practice.

The essential task in teaching is to get the student to behave in certain ways, and this behavior must be appropriate to, or appropriately controlled by, the subject matter content. This means, for example, that given a certain arithmetic problem, the student responds with certain solutions, or given a particular passage in a foreign language, he behaves by translating it correctly. The arithmetic problem and the foreign language words are the subject-matter "stimuli" to which certain student behaviors become attached. As a student goes through an instructional sequence, more and more appropriate and skillful behavior becomes attached to finer and finer subject-matter distinctions. In this way, student behavior is shaped from initial unskilled behavior to subject matter competence. Instructional programming is concerned with the techniques of how one goes about this.

There is another aspect of human behavior which must be considered as a basic premise in teaching. This is the fact that each individual has a unique history which shapes his individuality. Teaching can be most effective only if it adjusts to the singular requirements of each learner. Ideally the teacher and the learning environment should guide the individual actions of the student. The teaching of champions in sports results from the interaction of one man and one coach. The teaching of a skillful scientist results from the interaction of a graduate student with the individual professor in his laboratory. In the face of large-scale education and with the use of mass media, the skillful subtleties of the master teacher and the individualization of student instruction are often lost or reduced to an average method. Programmed instruction is attempting to increase the adaptive advantages of individual student-teacher interaction at the same time that the advantages of mass education are preserved. The present very early beginnings are only more or less successful in accomplishing this ideal.

Programmed instruction, then, is concerned with the selection and arrangement of educational content based upon what is known about human learning. It is a process of constructing sequences of instructional material in a way that maximizes the rate and depth of learning, fosters understanding and the ability to transfer knowledge to new situations, facilitates retention, and enhances the motivation of the student. It is an explicit process; it is what an effective teacher does intuitively. As this process is studied, the hope is that an effective instructional programmer might eventually be able to structure subject-matter instruction so that it develops according to definable rules that comprise a practicable teaching technology.

Instructional Objectives

A first and very important consideration in instruction is *what the student learns.* The primary objective of the teacher's work is to produce definable changes in student behavior and to bring this behavior under the discipline of the subject matter. For example, after instruction the student can make the response "8" to the expression "5 + 3." In this context the lesson to be learned from the experimental psychologist is a methodological one. In order to be appropriately developed, the learner's responses should be specified unambiguously in terms of tasks which he needs to perform. Such terms as "understanding" and "knowing" are amenable to experimental study and to instructional manipulation only when they are specified in terms of actual subject matter situations and observable student performance. While progress in the science of learning has been made in the experimental laboratory by such precise specification of behavior, there appears to be a general reluctance among educators to submit student behavior to analysis in precise terms. It is necessary that the objectives of instruction be defined not by such statements as "to acquire a basic understanding of earth-sun relationships," "to be able to solve problems in algebra," or "to understand the concept 'noun,' " but rather by such statements as "to differentiate correctly between such terms as 'revolution' and 'rotation,' " "given a linear algebraic equation with one unknown, the learner must be able to solve for the unknown without the aid of reference tables or calculating devices," or "to identify nouns by designating them in a series of words, distinguishing nouns in a sentence, or using nouns correctly in writing sentences and phrases" (Lysaught and Williams, 1963).*

In work on programmed learning it has been found convenient to make distinctions between *initial behavior, intermediate behavior,* and *terminal behavior.* Initial behavior consists of the behavioral repertoire the student brings to the instructional situation. Terminal behavior comprises the specified final set of accomplishments with which he is to leave the instructional course. The initial behavior brought to the instructional situation is the raw material out of which the terminal behavior will be shaped. It is therefore necessary to specify not only the eventual objectives of instruction but also the behaviors with which it is assumed that instruction will begin. The instructional materials or subject matter to which the student responds at the beginning of instruction are used to guide his

---

* Complete references appear at the end of each chapter.

responses in the direction of the subject matter situations with which he should deal at the end of learning.

In the course of the instructional sequence, between initial repertoire and terminal repertoire, the student performs activities which enable him to reach the terminal behavior or degree of subject matter competence specified by a particular lesson. The student activity that the teacher uses for this purpose can be called intermediate behavior. The teaching process seeks to use this intermediate behavior to reach desired educational objectives. This process is greatly helped by the detailed specification of the behavior that the teacher wants the student to perform. For each stage of learning, the subject matter stimuli (for example, words, symbols, and formulas) to which the learner can respond, and the kind of response which each of these requires (for example, solving problems, writing, or building a model) should be specified. In teaching mathematics, for example, is the student to solve problems, apply his knowledge to new problems, prove theorems, or all three of these? The construction of a learning program can differ radically as a function of the criterion behavior chosen. Furthermore, the activities the student performs must be specified in terms of observable behavior so that when such behavior occurs the teacher or teaching device can supply appropriate feedback, such as confirmation of the correct answer or correction. The necessity for the precise specification of behavior is hampered at the present time by an inadequate systematic terminology that educators can use to describe student behavior and also by the lack of psychological knowledge in analyzing complex behaviors. However, within the limits of present knowledge it is possible to apply concepts from the psychology of learning which permit more instructional guidance than is usually available in present classroom learning environments.

The topic of instructional objectives and what the student learns cannot be dismissed without mentioning those important extra-subject matter behaviors that are described by such words as "paying attention," "learning to learn," "curiosity," "concentration," and so forth. These also require explicit definition in terms of observable student behavior so that the teacher can recognize them, work with them, and subject them to manipulation by appropriate instructional procedures.

A programmed instructional sequence, then, takes into account the initial repertoire with which it begins and the terminal subject matter competence which the student is to achieve. Getting from initial behavior to skilled performance requires the manipulation of intermediate behavior, and the remainder of this overview chapter introduces several of the concepts currently employed in the construction of programmed instructional sequences for accomplishing this.

The Transfer of Stimulus Control

First to be considered is the transfer of student response from the stimuli of the initial repertoire to the appropriate stimuli required for subsequent performance. This refers to the procedure by which the behavior of the student becomes "attached" to subject matter content. Generally speaking, the process takes place in the following way: At the beginning of a learning sequence, the student is asked to make responses that are already familiar to him. As the learner proceeds to perform subsequent subject matter activities that build upon but are different from these, instruction takes place. In the course of performing these intermediate activities, the student transfers his original responses to new subject matter content and also attaches newly learned responses to new subject matter. This gradual transfer of behavior to new situations is what happens, for example, in Susan Markle's example of teaching vocabulary in a programmed sequence shown in Fig. 1. Here the word "around" is already in the student's repertoire and it becomes attached to or controlled by the new term "circum." This "around-circum" combination is then manipulated so that new combinations take place and new behavior is brought into the repertoire of the learner.

Sentence to be Completed	Term to be Supplied
1. The prefix **circum** (think of "circle") means "around." The circumference of a circle goes _____ the outside.	**around**
2. **Circumstances** are events going on _____ you when something happens.	**around**
3. A person who sails around the world _____ navigates the world.	**circum**
4. A cautious person **looks around** carefully before doing something; he is _____ spect.	**circum**
5. Which of these airplanes would fly farthest? _____ Least? _____ (a) interstate, (b) circumglobal, (c) transcontinental	**(b), (a)**

FIGURE 1. Part of a Program in High School Vocabulary.

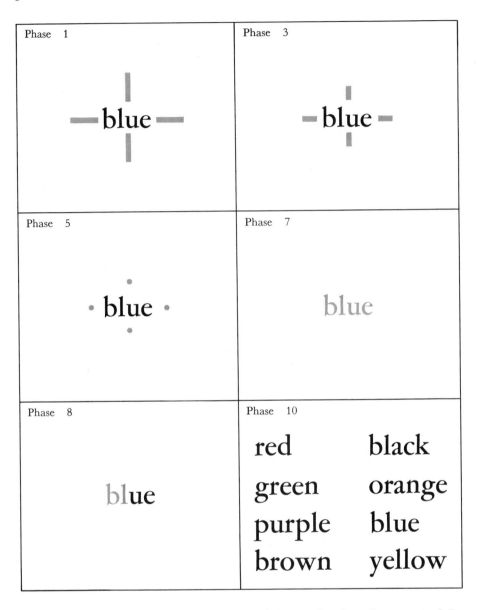

FIGURE 2. An Illustration of the Use of Prompting in a Programmed Instructional Sequence. Note: The blue coloring in the original program is represented here by the shaded portions of the figure.

Prompting and Guided Discovery

A second concept used in programming is called "response prompting," or, in certain instances, "guided discovery." The instructional procedure can begin by using only those responses which the student has available. The teaching task is to get the learner to make small changes in his responses which guide him toward the terminal performance. In a classroom and in a program, the instructional material provides a variety of situations which assist the student in making these small response changes. In other words, the instructional material prompts behavior which can be used to guide the student toward more complex behavior. For example, a young chemistry student learning the Greek prefixes for number might initially be prompted by having to complete such statements as: "A *mono*cle is a lens for use in only_____eye." Or to teach the prefix for ten he might be presented with the statement "The *deca*logue is another name for the_____Commandments" (Skinner, 1959). In a program in elementary physics the following statement might be used to help the student remember the meaning of the word "incandescent" after it has been introduced to him: "A *can*dle flame is hot; it is an_____ source of light." The response the student makes is the word "incandescent."

The use of prompting enables the learner to make, with a minimum of errors, the new, low-strength responses that he is learning. Prompting serves to make the occurrence of a response more probable and makes possible the design of an instructional sequence in which each learning step makes more likely the correct response in the next step. The use of such prompting, of course, must be based on the student's repertoire at a particular point in learning so that existing behavior can be used to prompt out new behavior.

While prompts serve to enrich the student's learning by helping him discover new responses, they are also necessary crutches which must be eliminated so that eventually the student responds to the subject matter content alone. Prompts therefore must be "vanished" in the course of the intermediate behavior that leads to the level of subject matter competence desired. As instruction proceeds, prompts are gradually withdrawn so that the student learns to perform and discover new knowledge without artificial prodding and with only the information or stimuli he will have available when he is to demonstrate subject matter mastery. The concepts mentioned so far can be illustrated by a short instructional sequence used for experimental study (Taber and Glaser, 1962). Figure 2 shows illustrative frames from a 74-frame sequence designed to teach eight color names to kindergarten children. The figure shows the portions of the program cycle for the word "blue"; this cycle was interspersed with similar cycles for other color names. Specifically, Fig. 2 shows how the word "blue" was taught through the program. The squares in the figure illustrate the form in which each of the eight color words appeared in phases 1, 3, 5, 7, 8, and 10. A child pronounced each of the eight words 11 times, and the order in which the words appeared varied from phase to phase. Consider this sequence in relation to the concepts introduced so far. First, there is a strong initial behavior: saying "blue" in the presence of the *color* blue. On the other hand, saying "blue" in the presence of the *word* blue is a weak or nonexistent response. The point of the program is to bring the oral response "blue" under the guidance of the word blue. The color itself initially prompts out the oral response in the presence of the to-be-learned word blue. The prompting crutch, the color itself, is progressively vanished so that the oral response comes strongly under the guidance of the word blue. This restricted example serves primarily as an illustration of prompting and of the transfer of stimulus control. The technique, in general, is applicable to a variety of situations. For example, a frame in a number-reading program may appear as shown in Fig. 3. Perhaps elementary reading training could be carried on with such words as "dog," "cat," and "dance" when the words are associated with pictorial representations of the real object or with figures illustrating the action referred to by a verb.

7

7 SEVEN 7

7

FIGURE 3.   The Use of Prompting in a Number-reading Program.

Gradual Progression

A principle implied in all that has been said so far is that a gradual progression of steps is employed in getting the student from his initial repertoire to the terminal repertoire. When developing complex performance, a programmed sequence first works with any available behavior which is the slightest approximation to the terminal behavior. In the course of instruction the student is guided by small changes which are in the direction of the terminal repertoire and is permitted, in a sense, to discover the next steps. In the course of this gradual progression, the attempt is made to make the student correct as often as possible, and complex behavior is built up through a graded series of steps. At each step the programmer asks what behavior the student must have before he can take the step and what general subject matter relationships or relationships to the student's behavior will facilitate making the progression from initial behavior to the specified terminal repertoire. The steps in the sequence are presented to the student only when he can encounter them with a high probability of success.

Reinforcement

A concept central to programmed instruction is "reinforcement." This is a concept about which there is much theoretical debate among psychologists, who are concerned with its various interpretations. On an empirical level, however, the influence of reinforcement procedures upon learning has been established. Reinforcement refers to the fact that the consequences of an individual's actions serve to modify and maintain his behavior. New behavior is learned or old behavior changed when the learner's actions produce a consequent event, such as a reward. Put another way, when an event that follows the learner's activity results in an increase in that activity, that event is said to be a reinforcer, and the process involved is called reinforcement. For example, when a parent makes sure that a child's desirable performance is followed by a cookie, the parent has provided reinforcement. Or, when the teacher makes sure that a child is permitted to perform an interesting exercise only when he has mastered some basic facts, he is in a sense providing reinforcement. The concept of reinforcement points out that individuals are influenced by the consequences of their behavior. Such events as praise, promotion, good grades, and wages which follow behavior can, therefore, serve to reinforce or strengthen preceding and on-going activity.

In the world in general, reinforcing consequences occur naturally as a function of the environment and society in which a person lives. In the classroom, the instructional process deliberately arranges behavioral consequences so that appropriate learning will occur. Programmed instructional procedures are set up to take advantage of the operation of reinforcement. One principle in designing programmed instructional procedures, then, is that provision should be made for specific reinforcement to occur. It is also necessary that reinforcement follow a response a sufficient number of times so that the response becomes strong and well learned. Practice without reinforcement is not very effective.

It is also known that the delay of reinforcement may result in little or no learning. In the design of programmed instructional procedures, this fact has been taken seriously so that the student gets almost immediate consequences of his work. In school learning, a major reinforcing event for the student may be "knowledge of results," that is, knowledge of whether or not the response he performs is considered correct. In many programmed learning techniques, such confirmation is immediately forthcoming upon completion of the student's response. The utilization of this fact of learning in educational technology is very dramatic in view of the frequent delay of reinforcement that occurs in many classroom procedures. However, it must also be pointed out that knowledge alone of the fact that he is performing correctly may be a less effective reinforcer for the student than being permitted to engage in further and more complex activity. His learning program can be arranged with this in view. Being able to move on, to get into and discover the fine details of the subject matter without being incorrect, frustrated, or punished for being wrong may be the most potent reinforcing consequence in a programmed instructional sequence. There seems little doubt that a significant aspect of educational technology is the management of reinforcing operations, and much research and development work is being carried out on the nature of effective reinforcing consequences for different subject materials at different educational levels and on the factors which affect the use of reinforcement.

Reinforcement must also be provided not only for subject matter knowledge *per se,* but for associated behaviors. Effective reinforcement can teach a student to learn to concentrate and pay attention to the subject material. When immediate reinforcement is forthcoming it appears that a student will be more likely to learn how to concentrate on specific features of a presentation. This is to say that the constant application to the subject matter which a program demands may not permit the development of competing habits of distraction; less controlled methods of teaching, however, may allow such behavior to occur more frequently.

Generalization and Discrimination

An important learning phenomenon that needs to be considered in instruction is that of "generalization." The term generalization refers to the fact that a student learns to respond to similar elements in different learning situations. He learns, for example, to recognize that all words with certain characteristics belong to one class called nouns or that all mammals belong to a class called vertebrates and many other creatures belong to a class called invertebrates. In addition to responding to similar elements in different situations, an individual also learns to make appropriately different responses to different stimulus situations. For example, he learns to discriminate between nouns and verbs. When a young child, on the right occasions, says "dog" and "cat," he has learned to discriminate between these two classes of animals. When he calls a strange cat that he has never seen before by the right name or when he says the word "cat" to the picture of a cat or to the sound of a cat purring, he has generalized within the class of stimuli that have something to do with cats. When an individual has learned to make discriminations so that he can respond selectively to different stimuli and when he has learned to generalize these same responses to a variety of situations, he has learned the concept. In the same way that the child learns the class concepts cat and dog, the older child learns the class concepts noun and verb, and the still older child learns the concepts light and sound.

The following example from the psychologist's laboratory indicates the kind of procedure used in many programmed instructional sequences to teach the student to make the same responses to all stimuli falling within a class concept and to make different responses to different classes (Mechner, 1965). In teaching a child who does not know colors the concepts of red and blue, objects are selected, some red, some blue, and some other colors. First, the child is shown successive sets of three objects, two red ones and one not red. Each time these three objects are presented the question is asked, "Which is not red?" This is repeated a number of times with only two blue objects. In this way discriminations are established between red and not red, and blue and not blue. The child might then be presented with two objects, one red and one blue and asked "Which one is red?" or "Which one is blue?" The number of nonred and nonblue objects could then be increased so that only one out of a number of objects is red or blue. In order to carry out training for generalization, objects with a variety of characteristics would be included in the sequence of color discrimination training—large and small objects, dark and light ones, rough and smooth ones, near and far ones, square, triangular, and irregularly shaped ones, etc. This would prevent the responses "red" and "blue" from being attached to stimuli other than the appropriate ones. With the properties of the objects varied, the child would learn to generalize among objects in which the common characteristic is color. In this way the child is presented with a series of progressively graded experiences by which he acquires the concepts of redness and blueness. Of course this is again a simplified example, and this process could be extended to the learning of many color names or concept dimensions having multiple categories.

While this process seems clear cut, it requires ingenuity to apply when the concepts to be discriminated and generalized become very subtle, for example, when the concepts classic and neoclassic art are to be taught. For this purpose it might be necessary to develop careful and lengthy discrimination and generalization training sequences. If students are to learn these concepts, it might be necessary to teach preliminary discriminations and concepts such as composition, subject, texture, form, and color tone. Another problem in teaching advanced complex concepts comes about when the classes themselves are imprecise and there is general disagreement among experts. It is difficult, for example, to teach the concepts of good and poor art unless one can define, at least among a particular community, instances about which experts would agree. It also may be highly desirable for an instructional course to leave the definition to individual determination and taste.

Understanding

Discrimination, generalization, and concept formation get close to the common-sense notion of understanding. When teaching machines and programmed instruction are discussed, teachers frequently remark: "Yes, the student seems to be learning, but does he really understand?" The answer to this question is related to the important fact that the educational technology underlying programmed instruction equates with behavior such terms as concept formation, understanding, and reasoning. This is so because the actual behavior that the student performs in the course of instruction is the only tangible evidence available that he is actually understanding and reasoning. It is up to the designers of instruction to provide problem situations which simulate instances in which the student must show understanding and reasoning. When such problems are devised and the student's behavior is observed and measured with respect to them, then it can be said that his performance is an instance of behavior which shows understanding or reasoning. The reply, then, to the question of whether the student really understands is, "Tell me what kind of behaviors, perhaps some test performance, that you would like the student to display so that you will know that he understands." When such terminal behaviors can be specified, it is the task of instructional technology to determine what combination of educational experiences will result in this behavior.

In general, it seems that continuous variations of the stimulus context in which the student responds result in the terminal behaviors which are defined as understanding, concept formation and utilization, and reasoning. These variations are set up so that the student gradually receives and discovers new information, learns to make progressively finer discriminations and appropriate generalizations, and also learns to apply his responses to a wide variety of situations. This process helps to enrich the student's breadth of learning and is an operational way of defining the development of understanding. Programmed instructional sequences can provide a series of well-organized examples leading the student to develop abstractions and complicated concepts. As pointed out by Skinner, "An important goal is to 'enrich the student's understanding' by inducing him to permute and recombine the elements of his repertoire" (Skinner, 1959, p. 65). The goal of instruction is really not concerned with the learner's response to any one situation. The objective is that the student acquire not a uniform and explicit set of responses about a particular concept, but rather a repertoire which is applicable in a variety of situations. He can therefore use the concept to solve problems, to describe a concept to others, to modify it for certain purposes, to build a model of it, to discover related concepts, and so forth. This terminal behavior can be defined as reasoning with, or understanding, a concept. Appropriately programmed sequences which can be employed with other kinds of learning experiences can provide the variation which contributes to the growth of understanding.

Empirical Development

An essential aspect in the construction of a programmed instructional sequence is that constant feedback about its effectiveness is obtained in the course of constructing a program. If a student does not learn, the attitude of the programmer is that something is wrong with the program and he attempts to modify it. The analysis, editing, and revision of this instructional material are based upon measurement of the student's performance, and the teaching procedure is modified on the basis of information obtained from the behavior of the learner. Each successive revision that is made in developing a programmed instructional sequence helps to ensure that the student's performance is brought closer and closer to the defined terminal behavior.

The work to date on teaching machines and programmed instruction is based upon the philosophy that the process of teaching and learning can be made an explicit subject matter for experimental scientific study and can form the basis for the development of a technology of teaching. As knowledge of the learning process increases, teaching can become more and more an explicit technology which can itself be definitively taught. The belief that teaching is primarily an art with which the gifted teacher has to be born and which defies precise description thus gives way to the conviction that teaching consists of techniques and procedures which can, in large part, be made communicable or teachable. This is not to say that the talent of the superior teacher can be replaced. On the contrary, it seems clear that outstanding performance in teaching, as in any profession, is achieved only by those who, in addition to a firm grounding in a communicable technology, bring to their practice a high degree of creativity and inspiration. This certainly must remain true in teaching as well as in medicine, law, architecture, engineering, physics, or musicianship. At the same time, however, the highest achievements in any profession seem likely to be realized only when they are built upon a well-developed underlying technology.

REFERENCES

Lysaught, J. P., and C. M. Williams. *A guide to programmed instruction.* New York: Wiley, 1963.

Mechner, F. Science education and behavioral technology. In R. Glaser (Ed.), *Teaching machines and programed learning, II: data and directions.* Washington, D.C.: National Education Assn., 1965.

Skinner, B. F. The programming of verbal knowledge. In E. Galanter (Ed.), *Automatic teaching: the state of the art.* New York: Wiley, 1959. Pp. 63–68.

Taber, J. I., and R. Glaser. An exploratory evaluation of a discriminative transfer learning program using literal prompts. *J. Educ. Res.,* 1962, **55,** 508–512.

CHAPTER TWO

Some Definitions and Operations in Learning and Instruction

From the point of view of the psychologist, learning involves the modification of behavior. The instructor's goal is to change the nature of the student's behavior with respect to a given subject, event, or object. His teaching techniques are all attempts to increase the probability that the student will make a particular kind of response to a certain subject matter. When the student has learned to add, for example, his response to "5 + 7" has changed from any number of inappropriate statements such as "5 cross 7" or "5 ex 7," and inappropriate activities such as scribbling or singing, to the appropriate response, "12." As a result of having learned to add, "12" is a response to "5 + 7" that has become highly probable or exists at high strength. Put another way, the stimulus "5 + 7" has come to control the student's behavior.

The primary contribution of the science of behavior to training and education is the premise that behavior is guided in this way by specifiable circumstances. While many of the characteristics of behavior and principles of behavior modification were first observed in the laboratory, it is the task of the psychologist interested in instruction to consider their application to human behavior outside the laboratory. This chapter and the next describe some behavioral principles which are useful both to the psychologist studying the behavior of his subjects and to the educator modifying and guiding the behavior of his students.

A major reason for including a discussion of basic principles in this book is that the technology of programmed learning is still relatively undeveloped. It is highly probable, therefore, that the techniques of programming will change to a much greater extent than the underlying principles on which they are based. Since the field is new and rapidly expanding, techniques must be kept flexible, and opportunity should be presented for ingenuity and innovation. The instructor who is familiar with the principles of behavior can make use of programmed instruction and other teaching procedures intelligently and effectively; instead of rigidly using certain instructional techniques, he can employ his knowledge of learning principles to integrate specific procedures into a generally effective learning environment. The exposition and explanation of principles of behavior should help make possible the optimal use of programmed learning and effective management of the learning situation.

The principles to be described here are quite general and need not be restricted to programmed instruction. The behavior of the student does not suddenly become subject to different principles of learning the moment he puts away his program or teaching machine. More efficient learning can occur with a good program in contrast to the ordinary classroom situation because of the carefully prearranged instructional situation that a program provides. Just as programs can be effective because of the consistent and well-planned application of learning principles, so the nonprogrammed situation, such as the tutor-student relationship, can be far more effective when the instructor understands the conditions which guide the behavior of the student.

Behavior as Observable Events

In a science of behavior and in a technology for education and training, the popular meanings of such words as "personality" or "conduct" are too general to be of use. The psychologist uses the term "behavior" to refer to the overt and measurable activity of an organism. The distinction between what can be seen of an individual's actions and what is inferred by an observer is especially important in the management of behavior. The overt, specific, and measurable actions of the individual are the data of a science of behavior and the building blocks of a practical technology. Through the study of observable behavior it has been possible for psychologists to begin to understand such complex forms of nonobservable behavior as problem solving and thinking. Similarly, in training and education it is through the guidance of observable actions that the instructor can influence such apparently covert performances.

STIMULI

A stimulus is any condition, event, or change in the environment of an individual which produces a change in behavior. Food may be a stimulus to eat; the command, "come here," may serve as a stimulus for movement; or the word "danger" printed in red letters may serve to abruptly change a person's ongoing behavior. A major task in building a programmed learning sequence is the careful arrangement of the subject matter stimuli to which the student will respond.

The term "stimulus" is seldom used abstractly but refers to a specific event which calls out specific behavior. A stimulus is that aspect of the environment which is responsible for producing the behavior; it is not necessarily that which appears to an observer to be responsible. For example, a child may "read" the word "yellow" by giving the correct vocal response when the word is shown, but the child may be responding only to the letters "LL" or "OW" alone. The child may have learned to respond correctly to different words on the basis of only a few features of each word. The teacher would be incorrect in assuming that the child responds to all those aspects of the stimulus situation which he as a teacher discriminates; identical forms of behavior may be caused by very different stimulus conditions. In an instructional situation it is usually best to assume that the learner attends to only those parts of the stimulus situation which are necessary for him to produce a correct response. If there is doubt about the nature or extent of the stimulus to which a student is responding, then the subject matter must be presented in a variety of ways so that the student's answers indicate that he is responding to particular stimuli or to a number of relevant stimuli at the same time. In brief, a stimulus is that aspect of the environment which guides or controls the behavior of an individual—"controls" in the sense of providing an event or object in the environment in the presence of which the behavior desired by the teacher is highly likely to occur. In the educational enterprise, the teacher manipulates the instructional environment in order to bring appropriate student behavior under the guidance of subject-matter stimuli.

The Stimulus Control of Behavior

When an individual responds in a certain way to a given stimulus, that stimulus can be considered to control behavior. The number of stimuli that control or influence behavior increases with maturity. The behavior of a very young child is determined by relatively few and primarily internal stimulus conditions, for example, hunger, pain, or thirst. As he matures, the child learns to respond to more and more external stimuli. The development of complex forms of behavior is possible because of an individual's increasing responsiveness to new sources of stimulation in his environment.

By means of learning, new stimuli are added to those which already influence behavior. Thus an effective learning sequence is an arrangement for the acquisition of new controlling stimuli to guide behavior. Since a technology of instruction is concerned with the manipulation of subject matter stimuli in the environment of the learner, an instructional process first requires the identification of those stimuli which currently control the behavior of the learner and then the placement of these stimuli under the management of the teacher so that the teacher can use the present behavior of the student to guide him to new forms of behavior.

RESPONSES

A response is a unit of behavior and the building block of complex performances. The flick of an eye and the twitch of a finger are examples of simple responses; eating, walking, speaking, and reading are all instances of more complex responses. A primary objective of educational technology is the guidance of an individual's responses. To accomplish this objective, the instructor must first define and enumerate the components of the performance, that is, the responses, that he wishes to produce. It is then possible to arrange the stimulus conditions which will result in the desired response. It also becomes possible to develop objective measures of the frequency and accuracy of the response.

The consequences of a student's response are extremely important in learning. The events which follow the occurrence of a response have an effect upon future behavior. Examples of such response consequences are reward, punishment, and knowledge of results. The reward or other stimulation provided to the learner immediately after responding is a significant factor which seems to determine whether learning takes place. The occurrence of certain consequences of behavior that are effective in producing and maintaining behavior is technically called reinforcement. In an educational situation, the instructor controls the consequences of the student's behavior. Since these consequences determine whether the student learns, the teacher will want to maximize those consequences which facilitate learning.

Approximating a Desired Response

The instructor's decision to reward or not to reward a student's response is usually based upon whether the response meets a specified criterion. In learning complex behavior, however, the student's initial response will be variable and quite crude and will rarely meet the instructor's criterion of competence. Effective instructional procedure tolerates the student's initially crude responses and gradually takes him toward mastery in small steps. This makes it possible to reward the student and have him experience success during the course of instruction. Teaching then involves establishing successively more rigorous standards or criteria for the learner's responses. For example, a person may take many attempts to toss a penny into a cup. In approximating accuracy, the size of the cup can be decreased gradually as accuracy increases. From the learner's point of view, any particular attempt is either a success or a failure. From the instructor's point of view, however, the standards set at any stage of learning provide results which have specific consequences for the learner.

One way to establish a new response, then, is by gradually contracting the permissible margin of error. If the goal, for example, were to teach precise tempo to a student of music, it would be unrealistic to reward the student only on those rare occasions when he briefly maintained a precise tempo. Since the beginning student will be quite variable in his performance of a task, standards should be initially gross. Performance criteria can be increased at a rate which keeps the probability of student error low. Each successive range of permissible or acceptable behaviors should include a major portion of the range of variations already in the student's performance so that there will be frequent opportunity to reward the student for successful performance. With time, the range of observed performance will align itself with the particular range of acceptable performance in force. As the student's behavior approximates what is required, it becomes possible to further restrict the criteria. A sudden and unrealistic constriction of performance criteria, however, is one environmental change which will immediately decrease the student's successes and, if sufficiently great, will result in the loss of student interest.

Response Repertoires

In actuality, any given behavior of an individual is complex and made up of many kinds of responses depending on the nature of the behavior and the level of skill of the individual. Several responses which are logically or functionally related may be grouped together and referred to as a "repertoire." Thus the responses involved in performing tasks such as typing, solving equations, or writing a sonnet constitute different repertoires of behavior. An individual's total behavior can be considered to consist of a wide variety of such response repertoires. The definition of just what behaviors will comprise a given repertoire in a given individual is determined largely by the objectives of training and education.

It is important to note that the terms "repertoire" and "knowledge" are not used here synonymously. For example, the meanings connoted by the terms musical knowledge and musical repertoire represent a difference in focus or interest. Repertoire emphasizes the behavior of the learner, while knowledge focuses on the subject matter itself and refers to its characteristics and content. Although musical knowledge refers to the vast body of information about music, a musical repertoire would be only a description of the behaviors demonstrated by a particular student of music. Thus the repertoire implies attention to specific behaviors which have been or are to be learned. A discussion of knowledge is generally concerned more with internal characteristics of subject matter than with characteristics of the learner's behavior. Because attention to specific behaviors comprising a repertoire is essential in programming and in teaching in general, this focus can be maintained through the use of the term repertoire.

Illustrative Kinds of Repertoires

In general, learned behavior consists of discriminative repertoires, the occurrence of which depends upon specific environmental conditions. Thus, as the term is used here, discriminative behavior refers to externally guided behavior. As an example of a simple discriminative repertoire, the child must learn to discriminate the situations in which "please" and "thank you" are called for. So must the physician learn the circumstances which require different treatment procedures. The identification or reading of different words is an example of an important discriminative repertoire in the human. In describing behavior it is necessary to consider not only appropriate desired responses, but also the circumstances (stimulus conditions) which should come to call out the response.

Many discriminative repertoires display a high degree of consistency in the order in which the individual responses in the repertoire are emitted. Skilled tasks, for example, often consist of sequential discriminations and performances which, due to the nature of the task, can occur only in a specified serial order. The assembly of a radio receiver according to a set of instructions and diagrams would be an example of a rather complex serial repertoire; a particular response in the series cannot occur until all preceding required behaviors have occurred. Typing from a manuscript is also an example of a serial repertoire in the sense that the typist follows a predictable sequence of text, as is done in reciting a poem.

Some important classes of behavior seem to occur without prior environmental cause; for behavior of this kind, there may be reason to suspect that the learner has become able to supply his own discriminative stimuli. Stimuli which arise from one's own behavior are often called response-produced stimuli. A learner who can sustain his own behavior through response-produced stimulation is said to be engaging in a self-sustained repertoire. The difference between reading and reciting will serve to illustrate this kind of repertoire. A person who has learned to recite a long poem is capable of engaging in a self-sustained sequence of behavior without reference to external stimuli and may be able to maintain the sequence uninterrupted in the face of varying environmental conditions. Each response in the self-sustained sequence is a stimulus for the subsequent response. Thus the occurrence of a self-sustained repertoire can be highly independent of environmental conditions.

The differences between discriminative, serial, and self-sustained repertoires often indicate differences in level of learning. The simple discriminative repertoire is little more than a recognition skill by which the learner is able to identify (respond correctly to) discrete elements of an external object, event, or situation. The serial repertoire assumes the ability to identify elements of the stimulus context but, in addition, the elements to which the student responds are serially ordered. The self-sustained repertoire includes both identification skills and past training in serial performance and also requires that the learner perform the serial tasks or discriminations involved without support from the external stimulus context. The individual in the process of memorizing a sequence of behaviors may initially refer to environmental prompts and cues which later are unnecessary. In memorizing a passage such as the English alphabet or Lincoln's Gettysburg Address, the learner becomes increasingly independent of the text. During memorization, control of verbal behavior is gradually assumed by the immediately preceding elements in the repertoire.

The term repertoire is used in other ways; for example, a "verbal repertoire" refers to what are commonly called language skills. The total verbal repertoire is further analyzed into smaller groups of responses such as speaking, listening, reading, and writing. These groupings are made on the basis of the similarity of the stimulus and response characteristics within each grouping. In contrast to verbal repertoires, motor skill repertoires refer to classes of behavior with different stimulus, response, and learning-process characteristics.

With respect to an instructional situation, an individual can be considered to have an entering repertoire and a terminal repertoire. The entering repertoire refers to whatever pertinent behavior the individual brings to the learning situation. The terminal repertoire is the behavior which the student should acquire from the instructional situation and is the reason for undertaking instruction. Usually, students bring at least some elements of the terminal repertoire to the instructional situation, and this behavior may be used in the teaching process to attain the instructional objectives.

Determining the types of repertoires to be taught in a given instructional situation serves to indicate the instructional approach required. Obviously, the training requirements for different skills will vary greatly: the ability to read and "appreciate" a poem is a very different skill from that of being able to recite a poem, and both are behaviorally different from the skill of stating the rules of poetic composition. If subject matter knowledge can be translated into the behavioral repertoires which it comprises, one is in a position to select appropriate instructional procedures.

REINFORCEMENT

The consequences of an individual's actions are critical in the modification and maintenance of behavior. Behavior is acquired (or modified) under conditions in which a response produces a consequent stimulus event (such as a reward) that strengthens or maintains that response. The stimulus event which the response produces is referred to as a "reinforcer" or "reinforcing stimulus." The occurrence of a reinforcer as a consequence of behavior is called reinforcement. When a parent makes sure that a child's desirable performance is rewarded or reinforced with a cookie (the reinforcer), the parent has provided for reinforcement. A specific response by the learner produces a change in the environment and this change, in turn, influences his behavior.

The arrangement of an environment that will yield certain stimuli (reinforcing stimuli) only when specified behaviors occur is the process of providing reinforcement. For example, in teaching a child to have good manners, a mother will smile whenever the child says "please" and "thank you"; in this way the mother reinforces the child with her smile. The giving of such a reward is a reinforcement, the smile itself is a reinforcer. Adult humans are similarly affected by the consequences of their behavior. Praise, promotions, grades, and money may all serve to reinforce or strengthen their behavior. In the example above, the child's correct responses reinforce the mother and strengthen her tendency to teach the child.

The reinforcing consequence of behavior may arise from the behavior itself, as eating cake leads to a pleasant taste, or may arise from the environment, as asking a question prompts someone else to give an answer. While most behavior consequences occur naturally, reinforcement in the educational setting can be a deliberately arranged consequence of behavior. A teaching machine, for example, is a deliberate arrangement for the student to gain immediate feedback for his performance.

The learner's response to the reinforcing stimulus. A most important general point about reinforcers is that they are stimuli. They are parts of the environment which are produced as a result of an individual's behavior. In addition, they are stimuli to which the individual makes a strong and rather consistent response. A reinforcer or reinforcing stimulus is effective as such precisely because it occasions a predictable and vigorous response. It is an animal's existing response to food, for example, that makes food an effective reinforcer in teaching other behavior. The strength of this existing response to a reinforcing stimulus is, in a sense, a measure of the power of the reinforcer to bring about further learning.

In the laboratory, a strong response to a reinforcing stimulus, such as food, can be assured by depriving the animal of the stimulus for a period of time prior to the training session. In a similar way, it is possible to assure that a human will find social approval rewarding by withholding such approval prior to its use as a reinforcer. Attention and approval, if lavishly given, become useless as rewards for good conduct. It follows from the above that a reinforcing stimulus may have differing levels of potency depending upon the individual's immediately prior exposure to it, that is, whether he is satiated or has been deprived. Over an interval of time, the effect of various reinforcers on an individual may be expected to fluctuate with the individual's prior experience with the reinforcing stimulus. Fortunately, the human learner is capable of being reinforced by a variety of circumstances, and an efficient educational procedure will attempt to use a rich variety of reinforcers.

Immediacy of reinforcement. In strengthening behavior, the effect of a reinforcer is on the immediately preceding behavior. Therefore a reinforcer must immediately follow the response to be learned. If the reinforcer is delayed, the desired response may never be learned (although other responses might be). A close temporal relationship between a reinforcer and the behavior to be reinforced is essential for the occurrence of learning. Efficient learning for a student takes place when the consequences of his behavior are immediately apparent. Especially when new, difficult, or infrequently occurring behavior is being learned, it seems essential that reinforcement should be as immediate as possible.

Characteristics of Reinforcers (Reinforcing Stimuli)

Reinforcing stimuli are frequently equated with external or environmental stimuli, such as food or expressions of approval. Reinforcing stimuli may also be internal to the learner, however. Many important rewards and punishments seem to be inherent in behavior. Often, for example, the process of responding seems to be reinforcing in itself—the individual shows "joy of doing." Thus the teacher need not always arrange explicit environmental reinforcers; simply arranging for the occurrence of a new behavior may frequently be sufficient to maintain that behavior for some time thereafter. More will be said later concerning responses themselves as reinforcers. In general, however, a reinforcer is any stimulation arising from the environment or from behavior itself which, as a consequence of behavior, may be used to modify, shape, or maintain performance.

While no single terminology or classification system is generally agreed upon by psychologists, for present purposes reinforcing stimuli can be discussed in terms of positive reinforcers, negative reinforcers, and punishers. Before their differences are compared, certain characteristics of reinforcers in general should be repeated. First, all reinforcers are stimuli which arise either from the environment or from behavior itself. Second, all reinforcers bear a close temporal relationship to the reinforced response. Third, all reinforcers elicit a strong and consistent response from the individual involved. Finally, reinforcers have an effect upon behavior and may be used to modify or maintain behavior.

Positive reinforcers. A positive reinforcer is any stimulus which an individual will "work to obtain." When produced as a consequence of a response, a positive reinforcer serves to strengthen and maintain the response. Examples of positive reinforcers include consumable stimuli such as food and water, as well as culturally derived stimuli such as praise and money. Immediate confirmation of the correct answer can frequently be used as a positive reinforcer in programmed learning. In addition to receiving immediate knowledge of results, positive reinforcers such as recognition of outstanding accomplishments, teacher praise, and the tangible products of a newly acquired response may also be useful in an educational situation.

Negative reinforcers. Loosely speaking, negative reinforcers are those unpleasant situations such as social disapproval or condemnation which the learner will readily terminate if given the opportunity to do so. When negative reinforcement is used, the response to be learned serves to terminate or eliminate the aversive stimulation. If engaging in homework is the only means by which a student can terminate the displeasure of a parent, the student may, over a period of time, learn to terminate this annoying stimulation quickly by engaging in the required tasks. Negative reinforcement, then, is a means of forcing behaviors to occur. Negative reinforcers are thought by many to be inefficient means of producing learning because they may force the occurrence of both wanted and unwanted behaviors. Moreover, undesirable emotional responses to an aversive situation may be difficult to modify when the situation itself is terminated.

Punishers. A punisher is an aversive stimulus which follows a response and frequently serves to suppress it. It is important to distinguish between negative reinforcers and punishers. Negative reinforcers precede the response and force its occurrence in order to terminate the unpleasant condition. In contrast, punishers follow the response and decrease the likelihood that the response will be made again. If disapproval or other annoying stimulation follows immediately after a behavior, punishment has taken place. On the other hand, when disapproval and scolding are directed at an individual in an effort to force behavior to occur and his behavior can terminate this condition, negative reinforcement is being used. Negative reinforcers and punishers are often grouped together under the term "aversive stimuli," since a given stimulus may often be used in both ways; the relationship to the response is the critical distinction between them.

Disapproval and condemnation given long after the occurrence of an incorrect behavior have little effect in weakening the behavior. Like reinforcing stimuli, punishment is effective only when it is relatively immediate. However, even with immediate punishment, the behavior may not be suppressed permanently unless punishment continues to be maintained. The research on punishment does not yet clearly indicate whether punishment can be trusted to have long-term behavioral effects except under special conditions.

In summary, some responses will be learned and others will not be as a result of the effects which the responses produce. By definition, a positive reinforcer is a stimulus which, when made contingent upon the occurrence of a response, serves to strengthen and perpetuate the response. Aversive stimuli may serve to force or to suppress, but not always to eliminate, responses. Punishers and negative reinforcers can seldom be used by themselves to point the way to other, more desirable forms of behavior; if they are intense they may hinder the educational process by suppressing all but avoidance behavior.

Secondary and Generalized Reinforcement

The properties of the various types of reinforcing stimuli tend to spread to other aspects of the learning environment in which they are used. Neutral stimuli which are accidentally or deliberately associated with a reinforcer may acquire the ability to reinforce behavior by themselves. The pleasant effects of candy, for example, may spread to the store in which candy is obtained or to the person who dispenses the candy. The psychologist distinguishes between stimuli which seem to be reinforcing, such as food, water, or pain, and those stimuli which acquire reinforcing properties through learning, such as money, praise, or criticism. Reinforcing stimuli which seem to be naturally or innately reinforcing are referred to as primary reinforcers. Derived or learned reinforcers are technically called secondary or conditioned reinforcers.

Just as the pleasant effects of a positive reinforcer may generalize to the environment, the effects of aversive stimuli may also generalize and suppress ongoing behaviors. When an individual is returned to an environment in which he was previously punished, nearly all his responses may be suppressed except those required to avoid direct contact with the aversive stimuli. After considerable exposure to aversive stimulation, such suppression of behavior may be brought about even by the suggestion that the learner return to the aversive environment. Thus secondary reinforcers, like primary reinforcers, can be either positive or aversive.

Typically, secondary reinforcers are the only ones available in an educational situation. Teachers make use of praise, grades, criticism, promotion, and fear of failure in order to modify student behavior. Numerous studies have shown that another effective reinforcer is receiving knowledge of results, i.e., being told whether a response is correct immediately after responding. Knowledge of results or confirmation, as it is sometimes called, is particularly suitable for an instructional situation and is often assumed to be the major reinforcer in present techniques of programmed instruction.

Education relies upon secondary and conditioned reinforcers which have acquired their effectiveness in shaping behavior through verbal and social conditioning. For example, early in life the child is exposed to combinations of stimuli in which primary reinforcers, such as sweets or toys which reinforce through permitting manipulative behavior to occur, are presented in combination with verbal stimuli. Thus the reduction of strong deprivations or aversive stimuli is accompanied by statements which the verbal community regards as "expressions of approval." Through such combinations of stimulation the child learns to be reinforced by such verbal events as, "Well done!" "Good job!" and "Excellent!" The child also comes to view any of his own behaviors which the community values and which is seldom observed in others as reinforcing, that is, he learns to be reinforced by his uniqueness or individuality and by any evidence shown that the community recognizes this. The community also uses the ability to engage in desirable behavior as a reinforcer when it extends permission or sanction for certain acts, "You may go and play now . . . ," or "Go on to the next problem since you can do this so well . . ." This rather complex history of verbal and cultural conditioning provides the child with a useful capacity for being reinforced in the educational setting.

Reinforcement in Education and in Programming

Positive reinforcement can facilitate instruction in that behaviors for which reinforcement is available will become behaviors in which a learner prefers to engage. Moreover, positive reinforcement often results in a general heightening of activity, which may be useful for instructional purposes. Praise, encouragement, and success seem to promote continued interest and enthusiasm for the learning task and perhaps the entire educational situation. In contrast, teaching through aversive stimulation, by means of disapproval or fear of failure, may lead to generally negative attitudes, and the learning situation itself may become something to be avoided.

Programmed learning is based on a philosophy which suggests the consistent use of positive reinforcement. In addition to knowledge of results, there are many other potentially useful reinforcers in programming, depending upon the characteristics and general background of the students for whom the program is intended. For very young children, being able to turn a page in a book may be strongly reinforcing. The instruction to turn the page and the ability to do so constitute a reinforcing event. Finding a short cut or an easier way to emit a certain response is also reinforcing for most learners. In programming as well as instruction in general, clever use should be made of all such reinforcers. The often heard dictum that being right is the sole reinforcer is too limited; a program should use as many reinforcers as the programmer can think of. In the context of teaching machines, additional reinforcers can also be found in clever techniques of automation.

It is not enough to provide a generally pleasant and approving atmosphere for the learner. He must "earn" the reinforcer. If rewards are dispensed without reference to the student's accomplishment, there is no knowing what behaviors will be reinforced and hence learned. Whatever behavior is in process at the time a reinforcer is given will be affected by the reinforcer. Thus it is essential to make reinforcement contingent only upon desirable performance. Further, a reinforcement is not a bribe. A bribe may be proffered before the desired behavior has occurred. If the person to whom a bribe is offered happens to be stalling at the moment, the promise of pay-off may reinforce or strengthen stalling. The essence of a reinforcer is that it is produced by, and is a consequence of, the learner's behavior.

A program will almost always be used within a larger educational environment and the program's effectiveness can be maximized by an understanding of how reinforcement is used in the larger environment. Some of the most potent reinforcing stimuli are social in nature, that is, derived from people. These social reinforcers are developed through the interpersonal relationship between the instructor and the student. However, the same principles of learning which give rise to efficient programs may be employed to make the interpersonal relationship more conducive to learning. When the instructor understands the proper way to use positive reinforcement and the way reinforcement affects behavior, he is in a position to make maximum use of a program and carry out an important role in mediating social reinforcement.

EXTINCTION

Extinction, or unlearning as it is sometimes called, refers to the process of permitting a response to go unreinforced. When a response is no longer reinforced it will occur less and less frequently and eventually will be eliminated. For example, a person who inserts a nickle into a broken stamp machine and gets no stamp for his money soon stops dropping nickles into the slot. In an instructional situation, lack of reinforcement, followed by extinction, can occur for many reasons: the pace is too fast, the difficulty too great, the teacher does not have time to give personal attention, etc. Lack of activity and lack of interest are symptoms of extinction caused by environmental circumstances that withhold reinforcement. Eliminating a response or a repertoire through extinction requires, first of all, identification of the reinforcers which are operating, since these are the agencies through which the response is maintained at some strength. Having identified the reinforcers, one is in a position to attempt to eliminate them so that the response involved will weaken and eventually extinguish.

The term extinction is used to refer to both the process and its effect. Extinction as an operation consists of removing or blocking the prevailing reinforcers. Extinction as a behavioral effect is the gradual decrease in frequency or likelihood of a response. The term may also refer to the weakening of stimulus control over a response. The phenomenon of extinction is of great importance to learning theory, but its practical implications for programmed instruction are less obvious currently than those of reinforcement. Some of the first teaching machines, those designed by Pressey during the 1920's, employed the principle of extinction to help students learn the correct answers to multiple-choice questions. Pressey's machines presented a series of questions one at a time and each question had several alternative answers. The machine had keys corresponding to the choices, A, B, C, etc. Pressing an incorrect key had no effect as far as the student could see, while pressing the correct key immediately reinforced the student by advancing him to the next question. Some modern teaching machines, automating the instructional process to various degrees, provide for the simple extinction of incorrect responses.

Extinction contrasted with admonition and persuasion. Verbal admonition, explanation, and persuasion are frequently used in education as attempts to guide student behavior in order to eliminate undesirable or incorrect responses. Such attempts may be effective when they prompt desirable behavior which can then be reinforced. Explanation or exposition by itself, however, is not a sufficient condition for the occurrence of learning. It is only when the learning environment makes the student respond actively to whatever materials are presented that the conditions for effective learning are approximated. On the other hand, if admonition and persuasion are used as negative reinforcers which the student will seek to avoid, they have little value in instruction. Generally speaking, a more reliable way of removing learned responses is to identify those aspects of the environment which reinforce the unwanted behavior and to arrange the environment so as to prevent these reinforcers from occurring.

Extinction contrasted with punishment. In the process of extinction, reinforcement is withheld with a consequent drop in response likelihood. In contrast, when a response is punished, a noxious consequence is produced by the undesirable behavior. It should be obvious that punishment and extinction involve very different operations and result in different behavioral effects. Consider the differences between the student whose behavior is met with a verbal reprimand (punishment) and one whose behavior is completely ignored (extinction). Reprimands and physical punishment often immediately suppress the punished response, but this suppression may be specific only to the immediate environment and may not be permanent. On the other hand, if an individual's behavior has not been reinforced over a series of occasions, it is less likely that the behavior will occur. Thus a student's misconduct in a classroom may be extinguished if he is ignored by everyone in the room. Punishment might only temporarily stop him from misbehaving.

Extinction and response substitution in programmed learning. In a learning program, the extinction process (the deliberate withholding of reinforcement) is seldom used as a separate procedure. The student is rarely if ever encouraged to engage in behavior which is left unconfirmed. If the student responds incorrectly to subject matter stimuli, one way to eliminate the incorrect response, of course, would be to withhold reinforcement. A more useful procedure with human behavior, however, is to teach a competing, desirable response to the stimulus. For example, most students begin algebra with considerable past learning in the use of letters in the alphabet. When asked what "x" is, the average student will answer that it is a letter of the alphabet; but in algebra the student must learn that x stands for an unknown quantity. Since the old response is desirable in other contexts, the algebra teacher or the algebra program will attach the additional response, "an unknown quantity," to the letter x rather than extinguish the old response. This process is called response substitution, and it appears to have much more practical relevance to programmed learning than does extinction as such.

SPONTANEOUS RECOVERY AND WARM-UP

Two phenomena which have been frequently investigated in psychological research and only occasionally referred to in programming literature are spontaneous recovery and warm-up. Following the extinction of a response the learner may again be placed in the extinction situation and, if some time has passed since the first extinction session, a sudden recurrence of responding is generally noted. This recurrence of an extinguished response is called spontaneous recovery. The name of the phenomenon is somewhat misleading since spontaneous recovery is predictable and often anything but spontaneous. The second phenomenon, warm-up, has been observed in studies of industrial productivity and human skill-learning. It refers to the frequent situation in which a person with learned skills performs in a relatively poor fashion at the beginning of a work session and improves in performance as the session proceeds.

The reliability with which these phenomena occur should be taken into account in the writing and administration of programs as well as in the management of the total learning environment. The programmer or instructor may easily succeed in substituting a new response to an old and familiar stimulus, but he should be prepared to find a student giving the incorrect response at some future time. Such an intrusion is similar to the spontaneous recovery of an old response. In any event, it is best to anticipate the possibility of intrusions in recently substituted responses by arranging appropriate review and practice sequences. Both extinction and response substitution are seldom complete in a single learning session and some amount of time, even if only a few hours, should probably be allowed to elapse between original learning and subsequent review. The same considerations apply in the classroom, where the instructor may successfully extinguish behavior only to find it return again at the next class meeting.

Both spontaneous recovery and warm-up increase with the amount of time the learner spends out of the situation. The longer it has been since extinction or substitution took place, the greater the amount of spontaneous recovery to be expected. Similarly, the longer a skilled operator has been out of his operating situation, the longer the time necessary to achieve maximum performance and hence the greater the amount of time required for warm-up. Basing a prediction on various studies of learning, it seems likely that the number of frames covered per minute by a student in a program will increase from the beginning of a session to a peak somewhere in the middle of the session, assuming the frames to be of equal difficulty. It also seems likely that the number of frames required for warm-up will decrease as the similarity of the materials covered in consecutive sessions increases. While traditional educational practice has been to terminate subject matter subunits at the end of a class meeting, somewhat the opposite practice may be indicated by what is known of the warm-up phenomenon. It may be that the transition between subtopics or units of the subject matter should occur in the middle of a session rather than between sessions, if the highest rate of progress is to be achieved throughout the entire program.

The foregoing implications regarding spontaneous recovery and warm-up are not the results of experimental studies with programmed learning materials. The appropriate research on such questions remains to be done. However, these speculations do point out that traditional practices may be changed as a result of considering the conditions necessary for learning.

It seems logical to divide programmed lessons into manageable units and to give the student some indication of the time he is to spend on each segment of the program. Although programming employs self-pacing, the learner can be given frequent convenient "stopping points." Each new program segment or lesson should begin on the assumption that old, incorrect, or undesirable responses to the subject matter may show some spontaneous recovery and that the learner will require some review in order to "warm up" and get back into the subject matter. The student who left his work at the end of Lesson 23 yesterday is not the same student who begins Lesson 24 today. Intervening activities are not without their effects and, indeed, are thought by most psychologists to be the real causes of forgetting, spontaneous recovery, and warm-up effects. Programmed lessons and instruction in general need to be planned to account for these phenomena.

SUMMARY

Major concepts and operations in the management of behavior are identified in this chapter. The principles discussed are relevant to the instructional setting as a whole as well as to specific instructional techniques such as programming. Some of the important points covered in this chapter are:

1. To the scientist and instructor, behavior refers to the overt, observable, and measurable aspects of an individual's actions. Learning involves the modification of behavior. The instructor's goal is to modify student behavior with respect to subject matter stimuli.

2. A stimulus is that aspect of an individual's environment that is responsible for producing a given behavior. The number of stimuli that control behavior increases with age, through learning.

3. A repertoire is a group of responses which bear some logical or functional relationship to one another. An individual's total behavior

consists of many repertoires. While any number of repertoires can be identified depending on the subject matter, some repertoires of general importance are: discriminative, serial, and self-sustained repertoires. A student's entrance repertoire is comprised of whatever behaviors he brings to the instructional situation. The terminal repertoire consists of the behavior which the student should acquire from the instructional procedure.

4. The consequences of a learner's actions are critical in both the modification and the maintenance of behavior. The occurrence of consequences of behavior that are effective in producing and maintaining behavior is called reinforcement. The term reinforcement refers to the process of providing such effective behavioral consequences.

5. Reinforcers are the stimuli produced by the learner's response. These stimuli may be positive reinforcers, negative reinforcers, or punishers. Positive reinforcers include reinforcing stimuli which the learner "seeks" or obtains by his actions. Negative reinforcers are those stimuli which the learner's response serves to eliminate. In contrast, punishers follow the response and subsequently suppress its occurrence to the particular stimulus.

6. Reinforcers are effective in modifying behavior because they themselves elicit a response from the learner. The strength of this response is a possible measure of the reinforcer's power to reinforce. A reinforcer's strength may exist naturally or may be acquired by learning.

7. The effect of a reinforcer depends on its immediacy in following the behavior it is to reinforce. With delays in reinforcement, learning may not take place, or undesired responses may be reinforced and learned.

8. Extinction is the process of omitting reinforcement and permitting a response to be unreinforced. In this way, a given response to a stimulus is unlearned or decreases in frequency. For instructional purposes, however, response substitution seems to be a more relevant procedure than extinction alone. In the process of response substitution, a new and competing response to a particular stimulus is taught.

9. Spontaneous recovery and warm-up are two phenomena which the instructor may observe occasionally. Both the recovery of extinguished behavior and the warm-up of skilled behavior should be given consideration in those instructional situations in which they may occur.

10. In the training situation, the instructor attempts to: (a) bring new stimuli to control the learner's behavior, (b) guide the learner's response to subject matter stimuli, (c) arrange for reinforcing consequences of behavior. In order to maximize positive reinforcement while the student

gains mastery, it may be necessary to tolerate approximations of the desired response and, as learning proceeds, to require increasingly closer approximations to the terminal behavior.

11. In general, programmed instruction is based on a philosophy of consistent, positive reinforcement, but the effectiveness of programming or any other teaching method is dependent upon the instructional environment in which it is used.

CHAPTER THREE

Stimulus
(Subject Matter)
Control of Behavior

The behavior shown by an expert in a given subject matter is characterized by quality, flexibility, and appropriateness, as well as by the facility with which the behavior is called out by particular subject matter contexts. Moreover, the expert's behavior is apparently self-sustaining; the expert may continue to respond for relatively long periods of time without the support from references that is needed by a learner. Put another way, the expert's behavior is made up of numerous self-sustaining and discriminative repertoires. He can make a great number of precise responses to many subject matter stimuli.

A course of instruction is an arrangement for a student to acquire the numerous discriminative responses that characterize expertise or "knowledge" in that subject matter; the student must come to display appropriate behaviors to the subject-matter environment. Another way of saying this is that his responses must come to be guided and controlled by the subject matter. As Chapter 2 indicated, a given response is "caused" or evoked by a particular stimulus. The phrase "stimulus control of behavior" refers to this fact. The present chapter is concerned with the operations which establish stimulus control over behavior. By means of these operations, neutral or previously ineffective stimuli are used to set the occasion for specified behavior. This manipulation, or stimulus control, of behavior is basic to instructional efforts. The term stimulus is used in this context to refer to the subject matter unit to which the learner responds. These may be small units such as phonemes and larger units such as words, phrases, rules, principles, concepts, strategies, and ideas.

DISCRIMINATIVE BEHAVIOR

That particular stimuli should come to call out particular responses is an assumption of nearly all training procedures. In the sense that the learner, in order to respond, must be able to distinguish such a stimulus from the general environmental background, it may be said that a control stimulus is a discriminative stimulus, one which the learner must learn to discriminate from other stimuli. The process by which subject matter or environmental stimuli in general are brought to control behavior is typically called "discrimination training."*

The phrase "three-term contingency" can be used to describe the relationship of factors which combine in discrimination learning (Skinner, 1953). The three terms or events involved in the establishment of a new discriminative response are (a) a stimulus for the response, (b) a response itself, and (c) the appropriate reinforcement for the response. The use of the word "contingency" indicates that each term or event is dependent upon the preceding term. The capital letter S is usually used as an abbreviation for the stimulus. When a stimulus is deliberately used in a discrimination training situation the letters S^D are used to stand for discriminative stimulus. The S^D is the stimulus to which the learner's response becomes attached through appropriate arrangement of the conditions which lead to reinforcement. A discriminative stimulus increasingly sets the occasion for a particular response because the response is reinforced only in the presence of that stimulus. A response is designated by the symbol R. The discriminative stimulus and its appropriate response are thus the first two terms in the three-term contingency. The final term is, of course, the reinforcing stimulus symbolized by S^R.

When the three terms are assembled in their order of occurrence in time they look like this: $S^D \rightarrow R \rightarrow S^R$. First, the stimulus for the response must occur; it may occur naturally in the environment of the individual or it may be deliberately contrived. Second, the appropriate response (R) must occur to the S^D and then must be immediately reinforced (S^R). The following is a simple example of a three-term contingency. In the cockpit of an airplane the warning light flashes on (S^D) indicating that one fuel tank is nearly empty and that a new tank must be called into service. The pilot responds (R) by throwing a switch which cuts the reserve tank into service. The pilot is reinforced—his behavior in this situation is maintained—by the termination of the warning light and the continua-

---

* In the following discussion the terms "discriminative stimulus" and "control stimulus" will be used interchangeably.

tion of the flight (S^R). Other people are also an important part of the environment, and in a social situation an S^D is provided by the behavior of another. For example, in the presence of a mother, frequently disposed to provide positive reinforcement, a child will learn many "outgoing" responses, while a punitive father or teacher may become the occasion for silence. Verbal material also supplies a rich source of control stimuli for both verbal and nonverbal behavior. The three-term contingency is a useful explanatory model, but its simplicity should not detract from awareness of the complexity of human behavior, just as the statement of a principle of physics in simplified terms does not make natural phenomena any less complex.

The precision or accuracy of the responses in the discriminative repertoire indicates the degree to which behavior is appropriate in a particular stimulus context; correct responses to arithmetic stimuli, for example, are obviously the most appropriate responses to the stimuli. Discriminative behavior is increased in precision by means of certain operations that vary the specific conditions leading to reinforcement. These operations can be simple, but result in a great complexity of behavior.

The following pages describe operations involved in the acquisition of discriminative behavior. For the programmer it must be reemphasized that these are the principles or operations which appear to underlie the way in which subject matter materials and task stimuli influence the learner's performance. The skill with which the programmer is able to apply such principles will in large measure determine the effectiveness of his program and the nature of his recommendations for integrating the program into a total curriculum. To a great extent these principles and practices are extrapolations from basic research and theory in learning and require further research and development to establish their further reliability. However, practical work with such extrapolations should facilitate the development of both instructional practices and research endeavors in the scientific study of behavior.

Establishment of Stimulus Control (Guidance of Learner Responses)

For a response to occur in the presence of a particular stimulus, the response must be reinforced when the stimulus is present. Reinforcement will serve to keep the response at high strength whenever these stimulus conditions exist. As previously indicated, S^D is the occasion upon which the response is appropriate and should be reinforced. All other situations are designated as S^Δ (S-delta) situations; S^Δ is any other stimulus situation which should not be the occasion for the given response. S^Δ might be a stimulus which evokes no behavior at all or evokes some different, competing, or substitute response. Since there are few subject matter stimuli which should occasion no behavior at all, what is S^D in one situation may very well be S^Δ in another. S^D, then, is defined by the teaching conditions of the moment; it is that stimulus to which a response is being taught.

In discrimination training, the correct response to S^D is reinforced in the presence of S^D but extinguished in the presence of all S^Δ's by withholding of reinforcement. Thus correct responses made during periods when the S^D is present are reinforced. Responses made when the S^D is not present (during an S^Δ situation) are not reinforced. Within the educational setting it is often more efficient to prompt the desired response to S^D than to wait for it to occur. This method might be used, for example, in aircraft identification training or in sight-vocabulary training. In the presence of a picture of a B-52, the correct response would be prompted initially by the written or spoken statement, "This is a B-52." Under these conditions the correct response would be almost certain to occur and could be reinforced. In sight-vocabulary training, in the presence of the printed word CHAIR a correct response would be prompted by a picture of a chair or the spoken word "chair." Other types of aircraft or other words should then be presented and any incorrect responses made to them extinguished by ignoring them. This is an obviously artificial training situation, since training would involve identifying all types of aircraft and many words, not just one. Therefore, a variation of discrimination training is of greater practicality in instruction because it results in the simultaneous learning of several discriminations. To take a laboratory illustration, an experimenter training a rat might arrange three colored lights—red, green, and blue—in the rat's box. Pressing a lever could be reinforced in the presence of the red light, a running response could be reinforced in the presence of the green light, and a string-pulling response could be reinforced in the presence of the blue light. This simultaneous conditioning method of establishing discriminations is a process often used in instruction. The individual who is learning to identify types of aircraft or words learns all types more or less simultaneously. At first the correct response to each picture or word configuration is prompted, then (especially in programmed instruction) the prompts are gradually withdrawn, leaving the responses attached to the pictures of words alone.

In summary, gaining stimulus control over behavior involves (a) training on a single discrimination with reinforcement of S^D behavior and extinction of S^Δ behaviors, or (b) simultaneous conditioning of different responses to different S^D's. The generalized discrimination training method can be diagrammed as follows:

$$S^D \rightarrow R \rightarrow S^R$$
$$S^\Delta \rightarrow R \rightarrow \text{Extinction}$$

Simultaneous training can be diagrammed as

$$S_1^D \rightarrow R_1 \rightarrow S^R$$
$$S_2^D \rightarrow R_2 \rightarrow S^R$$
$$S_3^D \rightarrow R_3 \rightarrow S^R$$
$$S_n^D \rightarrow R_n \rightarrow S^R$$

where 1, 2, 3, . . . , n refer to the different stimulus-response combinations being established. It should be noted that the process of extinction also operates during training in the multiple-stimulus, multiple-response situation. In learning different types of aircraft, a picture of a B-52 is an S^D for the response "B-52" but is also an S^Δ (nonreinforcement situation) for any other response such as "F-102" or "C-130." A picture of an F-102 is an S^Δ for any response except "F-102." Thus in both training situations any incorrect responses are extinguished.

In the preceding example, the separate responses to the different aircraft or words comprise a discriminative repertoire which is under the control of the aircraft pictures or word configurations used in the instructional situation. Subject matter stimuli cannot come to control behavior unless there is an opportunity for extinction to occur to S^Δ stimuli or unless competing responses are deliberately established to the multiple stimuli. When a particular behavior is always reinforced in one situation, but never in others, the learner will form discriminations more or less gradually over a series of practice trials. This process is very different from simply telling the learner to notice that a certain subject matter stimulus should make him behave in such and such a way. The active participation of the learner is a necessary part of the three-term contingency.

It may be helpful to use appropriate examples to point up the differences between programmed discrimination training and the more traditional method of teaching. Classroom instruction is usually verbal in nature, and the strategy of the teacher is designed to "inform" the learner that certain behaviors will be followed by a specified reinforcement contingency:

> "Hold the pencil as I do, and you will be able to make nice, round O's."

"You can always tell the difference between pneumococcal pneumonia and pulmonary tuberculosis if you remember that a positive blood culture is present in one and not the other."

"Do not shift to first (gear) until you have come to a full stop."

Teachers are often disappointed by this explanation-instruction strategy. Even with repetition, such instruction may have little effect if (a) the learner cannot discriminate the stimuli to which the instructor responds, (b) the verbal instruction calls for nonverbal behavior which the learner has not practiced, or (c) the learner is not reinforced by the events the teacher assumes are reinforcing. Furthermore, active participation alone does not guarantee that discrimination training is taking place. A teacher, for example, may ask a student to repeat certain words aloud as she points to a set of pictures hoping that with clever prompting she can get the learner to "associate" a response with a picture. But instruction and explanation become discrimination training only when the learner obtains distinguishable consequences for responding to the differences between stimuli to be discriminated. The crucial dimension upon which rats differ from mice, as far as the beginning biology student is concerned, is size. In order to train the discrimination between rats and mice, the educational materials involved must heighten the distinction based upon the crucial dimension and must provide an opportunity for comparison between stimuli. In a more advanced course in biology, the student may be asked to discriminate between rats and mice on the basis of more subtle aspects of anatomy or physiology. In a course in psychology the same discrimination, if it is made, might be based upon such differences between species as learning rate, auditory sensitivity, or instinctive response patterns. In every case, from elementary to advanced training, it is necessary first to specify the dimensions of difference to which the student will be expected to respond and then to make sure that training encourages reinforced responding *to the differences* (as S^D's) as well as to the subjects in isolation. Reformulating some of the examples given above, in order to heighten the discriminative quality of instruction, might produce the following:

"Now we will try holding the pencil in several different ways, both right and wrong, so that we can see which works best."

"In the following case histories you will find either a positive or negative blood culture. Check those you think to be cases of pneumococcal pneumonia."

"Now let's try shifting to first while we are stopped and while we are going five miles an hour so you can see why you should never do this when the car is moving."

The last example above illustrates how simulated instructional devices are often better than the real thing. If the reader will now generate a few examples in his own field of specialization he may readily come to see that there is a difference between discrimination training and such strategies as explanation, showing examples, and "capturing the attention" of the students.

Sharpening of Control

The preceding section indicated how a response may be strengthened in certain stimulus situations by means of reinforcement and weakened on alternate occasions through extinction or simultaneous conditioning. The control of a response by a particular stimulus may be further sharpened by presenting stimuli similar to the one which should evoke the response. By extinguishing the response to similar but slightly different stimuli and continuing to reinforce responses to the S^D, it is possible to train an individual to make increasingly more precise discriminations.

The tendency for stimuli similar to the S^D to call out the response to the S^D is a well-known fact of behavior called stimulus generalization. Often the learner's tendency to generalize the effects of training in one stimulus situation to other similar situations is a desirable end product of training. On the other hand, if such stimulus generalization leads to errors, further sharpening of the discrimination is indicated. This might be done by presenting similar but S^{Δ} stimuli and either permitting the student to learn different responses to them or extinguishing incorrect responses to them. With proper arrangement of reinforcing contingencies and stimulus materials, the human is capable of extremely sharp discriminations. Many technical and professional skills depend upon the existence of such refined discriminations. For example, the cues which tell a dentist whether a tooth may be saved or must be extracted may make little immediate sense when explained to a layman. Similarly, a skillful radar operator responds to subtle cues when discriminating between "targets" and "noises." In spite of the *apparent* complexity of such sharp discriminations, the physical dimensions of the stimuli involved are generally few in number. In skilled performance subtle discriminations can be based upon any one of many such stimulus continua: weight, color, temperature, size, duration, growth rate, etc. The process of sharpening a discrimination is concerned with increasing the individual's tendency to respond to small changes in the values of such continua. The results of sharpening are widely evident: the artist sees nuances in color never thought of by the nonartist, the physician responds to slight changes in a patient's heart rate, and the clinical psychologist becomes deeply concerned over behavior patterns unnoticed in the individual by others. As in training a simple discrimination, the first and most important task in designing a sharpening program is the identification of the basic dimensions of stimulus variation upon which the successful discrimination rests.

Extension or Expansion of Control

Once a response is reliably evoked in the presence of a particular stimulus, a second stimulus may be brought to control the response by presenting the two stimuli together and by supplying the appropriate reinforcement for extending the response to the new stimulus. The extension of the behavioral properties of one stimulus to another stimulus with which it is associated (physically, temporarily, and in terms of reinforcement) is a well-known phenomenon. Situations in which pleasant activities take place, themselves become pleasant. Similarly, the effect of unpleasant activity is often to make the situation one to be avoided just as the activity itself is avoided. In human verbal behavior, there are many cases in which different stimuli, often stimuli of a very different physical nature, must come to call out the same response. Words come to "stand for" concrete objects and to set the occasion for some of the same responses produced by the objects themselves. Whatever common behavioral tendencies are shared by word and object are products of discriminative extension in the past of the learner. Although one may never see a "real Communist," the term may be presented together with other stimuli which, because of prior training, tend to evoke certain comments and emotions.

Children who have learned to read can look at the word "walrus" for the first time and read it aloud with approximately the correct pronunciation. A child can do this without knowing anything about the object to which the word refers. If in the dictionary, for example, a picture or photograph appears together with the written label, the child may immediately "associate" the label with the picture of the object, given that reinforcement is contingent upon the extension. Very little training is needed to establish either the correct reading of the word or the useful relationship between the word and the object. The instructor's task is to arrange a learning sequence in which the child will become able to name the object without the support of the verbal label.

In most cases the verbal responses can be gradually extended to the pictures or objects over a series of trials or, in a program, over a series of frames. An extremely useful technique in extending stimulus control is "fading." Fading, in the example above, is the gradual elimination of the written label so that the learner is increasingly forced to depend upon the picture itself as a cue for the name, "walrus." Although the written label permits the student initially to respond correctly to the novel stimulus (the picture of the object itself), the programmer must eliminate dependence upon the label while also maintaining the correct response. Extension of control is very often the crux of a programmed instructional sequence. It is, in fact, the reason that prompts or cues can be useful. A prompt sets the occasion for correct behavior in the presence of to-be-learned stimuli; learning cannot be considered complete until the prompt has been successfully removed.

The extension of stimulus control along specifiable stimulus dimensions appears to underlie what is commonly called the development of a concept or abstraction. Abstractions and concepts are often thought to possess unique properties and to transcend the rules of ordinary behavior. One reason for difficulty in handling such terms is their lack of clear or specific referents. The word *apple* is appropriate (will be reinforced) only in the presence of a rather specific class of objects. *Fruit,* however, approaches the common formulation of an abstraction due, perhaps, to the fact that a far greater range of objects set the occasion for the response. There is even less inclination to call *comestible* a response to a specific stimulus. And yet, as a verbal response, a concept is most likely to occur to a specific stimulus condition: A physician says, "Here we see an example of *physical trauma* (injury) producing all the symptoms of a *contagious disease.*" A teacher wants to know of a student, "What makes this *animal* an example of an *extinct species?*" The abstractions shown above in italic type illustrate how common this kind of behavior is. Simply because such abstractions fail to suggest a specific stimulus object or event does not seem to be adequate reason to suppose that concepts and abstractions transcend stimulus-response analyses.

A concept does not exist independently of the people who use it. Behavior attributed to concepts can usually be shown to exist at some strength because of past reinforcement to specific situations. A teacher

TABLE 1

Name of concept	Relevant behaviors (verbal statements)	Critical dimensions or qualities of the stimulus
Circle	"The movement of planets is circular." "The circus gets its name from the gladiatorial ring." "These objects form a circle . . ."	A closed plane curve consisting of all points equally distant from a point, the center.
Brightness	"Silver is bright, lead is dull." "How bright the moon is!"	The amount of light energy reflected or emitted by any object.
Noun	"The subject of a sentence may be a noun or a noun cluster." "Cincinnati, Shakespeare, and Buckingham Palace are proper nouns." "That sentence contains a noun, a verb, and two adjectives."	A word that is the name of a subject of discourse, as a person, thing, quality, idea, or action.

does not apply certain methods of teaching because "concepts of modern teaching" guide his behavior, but either because certain strategies work better than others or because supervisors tend to selectively reward and punish different strategies. That people behave "as if" abstractions were guiding their behavior is the outcome of a history of reinforcement contingencies with respect to specific stimulus situations. Concepts, then, must depend for their definition upon (1) the behaviors which reflect the attainment of the concept and (2) the qualities in the stimulus situations involved which are critical to the occurrence of an appropriate response. Table 1 shows examples of this formulation.

A concept may be learned through a process of discriminative stimulus extension which arises from an instructional sequence in which actual objects or verbal stimuli represent those objects. Whether a concept is to be taught through exposing the learner to a program of variations in stimulus properties of objects or events, through exposure to a planned sequence of verbal behavior, or through a combination of both is a decision brought about by many factors, but one which is made deliberately and in advance of a programmed instructional situation.

Special difficulty is encountered with concepts such as "truth," "freedom," or "honesty" because they are particularly subtle. They are, moreover, in the process of constant change and formulation by individuals and groups. The range of behaviors which signify the attainment of such concepts poses unique problems in defining educational objectives. Frequently such behavior is verbal since it is difficult to see a man behaving nonverbally "as if he knows what truth is." Also the verbal expression of the concept frequently contains the verbal name for the concept: "There is truth in what you say," "In the world of free men . . . ," or "John is an honest person." It might be said that John is honest because he acted honestly in a given situation, but this avoids a description of the characteristics of the situations which lead to the development of his behavior. With recognition of the limitations of the present analysis, a concept, as defined here, is a set of responses developed by the reinforcing environment to specified stimulus properties which vary in certain ways. The controlling stimuli may be verbal or nonverbal, and what is required for instructional purposes is a specification of the extent and nature of permissible variation in stimulus properties. Sometimes the dimensions of the environment which are to eventually control behavior relevant to certain abstractions cannot be well specified and must be taught. It is still necessary, under such circumstances, that the teacher select illustrative experiences which he interprets as stimulus situations which will develop the concept involved.

Consolidation of Controls

A particular verbal response can refer to an entire class of stimuli as, for example, when a group of dissimilar organisms are all classified as animals. In education, it is frequently desirable to combine independently strengthened discriminative responses under the control of a single stimulus condition. Thus the separate responses "bear," "dog," "horse," and "chicken" would all be placed under the control of the more general stimulus, "animal." This process is often called teaching a rule, and it illustrates the consolidation of a number of learned discriminations. Consider the statement, "All of the plaster models in this case are models of mammals; point out what it is about each that makes it a mammal." A similar statement might be, "Let's speak Spanish now; pronounce the vowels as they are pronounced in Spanish." The use of the words "mammals" and "Spanish" assumes that these words call forth certain discriminative repertoires. A large part of what is called "understanding of a subject matter" appears to consist of precise discriminative repertoires which have themselves come under the guidance of appropriate more general stimuli, such as a concept or a rule.

The consolidation of control is a means of assuring that competing repertoires do not interfere with each other and that behavior has the degree of flexibility necessary in a changing environment. The mention of the word "mammals" to a biology student increases the probability of a large group of responses. The suggestion that the class is going to discuss a group of animals called mammals raises an appropriate discriminative repertoire to high strength, while many other responses which could be appropriate in biology classes are weakened. In other words, the students are ready to discuss mammals, not insects or fish. Since the understanding of a rule is a frequent goal in education and training, it would seem worthwhile for a programmer or instructor to provide training in the appropriate use of different rules. This can be done by alternating between instructional segments which call for the use of different rules so that the student has an opportunity to discriminate his own behavior in different circumstances.

The processes of establishing and modifying stimulus control have been presented in terms of two fundamental operations: reinforcement and nonreinforcement. The particular operations described for manipulating stimulus control illustrate some general classes of learning situations. From the strict point of view of learning theory, the notions discussed may be both incomplete and overlapping. From the programmer's point of view, it may be difficult to keep all of the methods for manipulating stimulus control in mind while also concentrating on subject matter and its arrangement into an instructional sequence. However, the programmer who is familiar with the principles of discrimination learning will find that his programming technique has a degree of flexibility and adaptability that is difficult to acquire without an understanding of the basic principles of learning.

Discrimination and Differentiation

Thus far the discussion has centered on external stimuli in the presence of which a response occurs. In a similar manner, however, responses may in some instances be prompted by feedback from preceding responses, rather than by stimuli in the external environment. Skillful motor responses, such as working a lathe or pitching a ball, involve a sequence of internally controlled movements in which, presumably, each response serves as the stimulus for the next response. In the course of learning such skillful behaviors, an individual's responses become increasingly more precise as training proceeds. The learning process whereby these behaviors increase in precision is called differentiation, and a skillful response itself is called a differentiated response. For differentiated responses, sensory stimuli from the muscles, tendons, and skeletal joints determine further muscular movements. In general, the learning of motor skills (as opposed to perceptual-verbal skills) involves the process of response differentiation.

In differentiation training, it is primarily the *way* in which the differentiated response is executed—the specific form of the response—that determines whether reinforcement is given or withheld. However, when the terminal repertoire is a finely differentiated response, that is, highly specific and precise, the probability of *incorrect* responses occurring during training is great. There is even danger that all behavior may eventually be extinguished if careful approximations to the terminal behavior are not used. The notion of permissible standards, mentioned in Chapter 2, is of great utility in approximating a skilled response. For early approximations of a motor skill, standards must be quite broad so that reinforcement is frequent. As performance becomes coincident with one range of tolerances, tolerances should be contracted slightly to produce a further improvement in performance. Thus differentiations, like discriminations, can be programmed and taught in gradual stages through approximations (although much less work has been performed on programming motor skills than has been carried out for verbal behavior).

Examples of differentiated behaviors include learning to aim a rifle to hit a target, learning to pronounce a letter so that the sound is similar to that acceptable in the verbal community, and learning to bowl with accuracy. In contrast, some skills that primarily involve discrimination are learning to read printed words, learning to use a slide rule, and simply learning to tell the difference between a circle and a square. Many activities include discriminations of external situations and differentiations of precise muscular movements as well, for instance, playing a musical instrument, dancing, and writing in longhand.*

---

* Some psychologists consider differentiation a form of discrimination training in which the S^D's involved are kinesthetic muscular and skeletal stimuli. But for the purposes of this book the distinction between discrimination and differentiation seems to serve to point up an important emphasis on the stimulus and response aspects of instructional practice.

Since the stimuli which facilitate the occurrence and reinforcement of a differentiated response arise from the response itself, it is very nearly impossible, with present techniques, to determine the specific nature of these private stimuli. As a result, the instructor has no direct way of manipulating stimuli that produce a sequence of skilled muscular movements. However, he can make the desired response more probable by means of verbal directions and by other environmental arrangements that heighten the likelihood of correct performance. For example, in teaching swimming, a harness around the student may be used so that the instructor can have effective observation and guidance of the student's form. In addition to arranging the environment to maximize performance, the teacher can use the notion of approximations. The boy learning to pitch a baseball should initially be expected to throw it accurately for a shorter than standard distance, and the beginning bowler might be started out on a short alley. As proficiency increases, the distance (standards, in a sense) should be gradually increased to conditions which are generally required in working with the skilled task that is eventually to be learned.

Self-Observation

Frequently, the process of differentiating the form of a response can be facilitated by first teaching the student to discriminate the desired form of the responses when made by other people. It is often easier to learn to perform a specific skilled act if the learner knows how the act should look or sound. It would seem difficult, for example, to learn to play the piano really well without ever having heard good pianists; certainly it would seem to require a longer period of training. In general, when discrimination of the correct form of behavior precedes differentiation of that behavior, instructional time may be saved. If an individual who is to learn a differentiated response has first been taught to discriminate a good performance from a poor one in others, it then becomes possible to teach "self-discrimination" so that he may become his own observer and evaluator. Teachers frequently have to call the learner's attention to what he is doing wrong, the learner being unable to make the discrimination himself. "Self-observation," however, is a class of behaviors (discriminations) which can be strengthened with effective reinforcement. Thus an "ideal" program for teaching skilled performance would contain instruction in (1) verbal and nonverbal subject matter knowledge, (2) the training of discrimination between good and poor performance elements in others who are working at the same task, (3) reinforced error detecting or self-observation, and (4) further practice of the skill in a variety of contexts and with modifications. If the learner is to become independent and self-correcting, then training in self-discrimination is of appreciable importance. An important consequence of such training is the enhancement of the inherent rewards for the student in working toward a perfect performance. It is interesting to consider such academic subject matters as second language training, music, drawing and painting, and laboratory techniques in the light of the above notions.

Most current efforts in programmed learning involve discrimination training using verbal or symbolic subject matter stimuli. Such verbal programming is the primary concern of this book. However, the distinction between discrimination and differentiation is important because it calls attention to the learner's response. It has been pointed out that in verbal programming the programmer may start with very rough discriminations of different terms, principles, and rules. These discriminations become increasingly fine and of greater number as the program progresses. In addition to the elaboration of discriminations, however, the program must lead the student to larger and larger segments of behavior which are relatively free of external prompting. A verbal-symbolic program, then, is usually best designed when it differentiates, or leads to the production of, increasingly complex self-sustained behavior. Some programs which are not designed to produce the highest levels of ability in the student may never require more than a one- or two-word response. However, a program that claims to teach mastery of a subject should generally call for larger and complete statements from the student as training proceeds.

In summary, discrimination training directs attention to the stimuli in the learning situation. Discriminations may be approximated by gradually reducing the differences between the stimuli to be discriminated while the total number of stimuli and associated responses is increased. Differentiation training, on the other hand, calls attention to the form or features of the behavior itself. Differentiations may be approximated by gradually requiring more and more precise responses. Approximations of both discriminations and differentiations involve a slow reduction of the variation in acceptable behavior. Optimally, both discrimination and differentiation training depend upon a number of factors: selective reinforcement, extinction of incorrect performances, successive approximations, and a high frequency of reinforcement for correct responses, the definition of correct being constantly subject to change.

STIMULUS GENERALIZATION

When a response to a particular stimulus is reinforced, the likelihood is increased that the response will also occur to similar stimuli. The tendency of similar, but not identical, stimuli to call forth previously learned behavior is called stimulus generalization. Students who have learned about a simple one-cylinder internal combustion engine are very likely to call any other engine that operates by combustion of compressed vapors an internal combustion engine regardless of the type of fuel used, the number of cylinders, or the use which is made of the engine. Although this example illustrates complex behavior, it is similar to the simpler phenomena found under laboratory conditions. Generalization can be obtained by establishing a response to a specific stimulus through training and subsequently eliciting the same or a similar response after slight changes have been made in the original stimulus. The greater the change in the stimulus, the less likely it is that the learner will make the response. Conversely, the more similar the stimuli along which the learner must discriminate, the more likely it is that he will confuse the stimuli and, therefore, the more precise and deliberate must be a discrimination training procedure.

Often the stimuli in the learner's environment are highly complex and consist of intricate stimulus patterns. The term "abstraction" is frequently applied to discriminative behavior which seems to be directed by a set of complex stimuli. For example, the term "animals" is an abstraction made in response to a class of stimuli in which responses to the specific elements of the complex stimulus (the characteristics of organisms) have been generalized over a variety of different species. In beginning biology the student is taught to see similarities between one-celled animals and man; for example, both man and amoeba convert types of energy, excrete, reproduce, move about, and cannot live without certain substances. Each of these common characteristics can be considered an abstraction. Although the specific stimuli involved, men and one-celled animals, are extremely divergent, the competent student of biology makes certain common responses to all objects in the stimulus class called animals because he can discriminate properties common to all.

If the commonality of his behavior to diverse objects is not pointed out to the student, it may be a long time before he makes the induction himself. Induction from particular instances to general principles is the method by which scientists form abstractions, but this sometimes may be too difficult a process for the student. Moreover, it is probably often wasteful to force the student to rediscover all the abstractions of a subject matter. Instead, the commonality of established behavior may be pointed out to him and presented as a discriminative stimulus. Following this, the advanced student must be able to discriminate the properties of his own behavior to newly observed stimuli so that he can transfer his abstraction and extend it in order to form inductions and generalizations on his own.

Stimulus generalization is not always a desirable product of training. Often the learner will generalize his responses to incorrect stimuli. Learners may either overgeneralize or undergeneralize, and if they are left to their own devices there is no assurance that they will respond appropriately to a new class of stimuli. Implicit in the preceding sections on discrimination is the notion that the trainee should not be left unguided, at least during the early and middle stages of training.

If the learning environment is not carefully structured, it is likely that incorrect generalizations will be reinforced. Programmed instruction offers an opportunity to inspect and test subject materials prior to teaching so that the extent and amount of discrimination and generalization training may be assessed. A sequence of steps designed to teach generalization, for example, can be tried out on subjects to determine its effectiveness. Careful evaluations of student performance as a result of the instructional program permit objective conclusions about whether a program or sequence achieves its goal of generalization; if it does not, the program can be rewritten appropriately and retested prior to widespread use.

If generalization or the absence of it is a critical goal of teaching, an instructional program should include appropriate sequences of frames to insure the precision of the resulting discriminations or the breadth of subsequent generalizations. Such general principles as the sharpening and extension of subject matter control are relevant in this connection and may be translated into specific programming procedures such as those outlined in Chapters 5 and 6.

RESPONSE CHAINING AND THE INTEGRATION OF BEHAVIOR*

A chain of responses is a sequence of responses in which each member of the sequence has discriminative properties (acts as an S^D) for the subsequent members. A response in a chain is both a response to the

---

* Textbook discussions of response chaining are presented in Holland and Skinner (1961), Homme and Klaus (1961), and Keller and Schoenfeld (1950). A detailed treatment of the applications of response chaining to practical instructional situations is found in Gilbert (1962a; 1962b).

preceding stimulus and a discriminative stimulus for the next response. The final result of a chain of behaviors is the reinforcing event at the termination of the chain—it is the primary reason why the chain exists at all in the learner's repertoire. Because of this, a chain of behaviors which culminates in reinforcement is considered as a functional unit.

Many subject-matter tasks are integrated chains of responses. Expert behavior is performed in a smoothly flowing sequence, as the discussion of "self-sustained" repertoires in Chapter 2 has emphasized. At the end of a phase of instruction the terminal behavior often desired of a student in a given subject matter is the ability to perform chains of behavior. Throughout their schooling, students acquire many chains of verbal behavior from reciting the alphabet or counting to learning multiplication tables, poems, stories, or chemical formulas. Such chains are usually taught by starting with the first element or first few elements of the chain and moving gradually towards the end of the chain. For example, children are taught the alphabet in the order A, B, C, D, E . . . It is common practice in much experimental work with animals to teach a chain of behaviors by beginning at the end of the chain. In the laboratory, training a chain of behaviors usually begins with the last-to-occur member of the chain, and proceeds in a *backward* fashion towards the first-to-occur member of the chain. That is, the order in which the chain is taught and the order in which it is performed are opposite. The reason for this procedure is that the terminal response of the chain is the response which eventuates in reinforcement or which is instrumental in producing the reinforcer.

The Laboratory Paradigm of the Response-Chaining Process

A simple chain of behaviors in the rat such as pulling a loop of string, followed by pressing a lever and then eating from a food magazine, has often been used in demonstrations of chaining. In this situation, the rat is first trained to eat from a food tray which makes a click or some other sound as it opens. The effects of the food generalize to the sound of the tray and the sound becomes a secondary reinforcer as well as a cue for the presence of food in the tray. After the rat has learned to approach and eat food from the tray, the sound of the tray is used to reinforce the lever-pressing response. When the rat presses the lever, the food tray click is presented immediately, reinforcing lever pressing and signaling the presence of food. Thus the tray click is also a discriminative stimulus for a response of moving away from the lever and towards the food tray.

The general procedure for chaining with animals requires that each member of a response chain be placed under discriminative control while it is established, just as the approach to the food tray was placed under the discriminative control of the click. The lever-press response is generally placed under the control of some external stimulus such as a light. When the light comes on, any lever presses will be reinforced with the click. After discriminative control of the lever press has been established so that the light reliably occasions a response, the third member of a chain (pulling a loop) may be established. Thus when a response to the loop occurs, the light is turned on, reinforcing the loop-pull and also setting the occasion for the lever-press response. The loop-pulling response may in turn be placed under discriminative control so that a buzzer, for example, signals the occasion for the loop-pulling response. At the sound of the buzzer, the loop-pulling response occurs resulting in the light being turned on, after which the lever press occurs, and so forth through the remainder of the chain.

As Chapter 2 indicated, reinforcing stimuli are also discriminative stimuli which lead to a response; therefore, one defining property of a reinforcing stimulus is the strong and consistent response it evokes from the learner. In chaining, stimuli are used both to reinforce the preceding response as it occurs and to set the occasion for the subsequent response. In the chain of behaviors just described, the click of the food magazine reinforces lever pressing because the click has been associated with or led to food in the past. The click also becomes the S^D for approaching the food magazine. Similarly, the light is used to reinforce loop pulling and to set the occasion for the lever press. Symbolically, the responses involved look like this:

$$\text{Buzzer} \qquad\qquad \text{Light} \qquad\qquad \text{Click} \qquad\qquad \text{Food}$$

$$\begin{bmatrix} S_4^D \\ \end{bmatrix} \to R_4 \to \begin{bmatrix} S_3^D \\ S_3^R \end{bmatrix} \to R_3 \to \begin{bmatrix} S_2^D \\ S_2^R \end{bmatrix} \to R_2 \to \begin{bmatrix} S_1^D \\ S_1^R \end{bmatrix} \to R_1$$

$$\uparrow \qquad\qquad \uparrow \qquad\qquad \uparrow \qquad\qquad \uparrow$$

$$\text{Loop} \qquad\quad \text{Lever} \qquad \text{Approaching} \qquad \text{Eating}$$
$$\text{pull} \qquad\quad \text{press} \qquad\quad\; \text{food}$$

R_1 is the eating response to food, R_2 is the approach to food, R_3 is the lever press, R_4 is the loop pull. Actually, many other behaviors at various levels of specificity are involved. Each chewing movement might, for example, be treated as a separate response and certainly the reader may wonder why the response of approaching the lever is not included. The diagram is intended only to symbolize the chain, however.

The parenthetical terms in the diagram indicate the external stimuli: (1) sight or smell of food, (2) food tray click, (3) light, and (4) buzzer. The buzzer, S_4^D, only sets the occasion for the loop pull and is not used to reinforce any previous behavior. The other stimuli are labeled with the two sets of symbols, S^D and S^R, to stress their dual function as reinforcers as well as discriminative stimuli. The reinforcing value of all the stimuli in the rat's situation, with the possible exception of food itself, is obviously learned during the training process. These learned reinforcers were originally neutral stimuli which acquired their reinforcing properties through association with food, the primary reinforcer.

In the diagram of the chained sequence, the numbers refer to the order in which the response and associated discriminative stimuli were established or taught. The arrows, on the other hand, indicate the temporal direction or flow of behaviors when the chain is performed. The order in which behaviors were taught to the animal and the order in which the final chain occurs are exactly opposite.

Having trained an animal in this particular performance sequence, the trainer must expect that the entire chain will occur as frequently as the buzzer (the initial S^D) is turned on. The occurrence of the sequence is thus under the control of the trainer. The light for the lever press and the click for the food response are also external stimuli that have come to control the rat's performance. If the light and the click are eliminated abruptly the animal may take an increased amount of time to complete the chain. The effect may be only temporary, but in very long performance chains the disruption of behavior may so delay the final reinforcement that extinction takes place. If the intensity of the light and the click are diminished gradually over a series of trials, however, performance may be maintained at a high rate while it is being made independent of environmental cues. At the completion of the final stage of training the rat's performance could be diagrammed as follows:

$$(S_4^D) \to R_4 \to R_3 \to R_2 \;\to\; \begin{bmatrix} S_1^D \\ S_1^R \end{bmatrix} \;\to R_1$$

The initiating control (buzzer, S_4^D) and the sight and smell of food (S_1^D, S_1^R) remain, but the light and the click have been eliminated. The rat's own behavior has taken over the role of the removed stimuli so that pulling the loop has become the stimulus for pressing the bar. Similarly, a lever press has become the stimulus for approaching food. In short, it is possible to make the behavior of the animal itself both reinforcing and discriminative. In terms of this particular chain of behavior, the rat has become a self-sufficient expert. He can now reel off complex behavior in a smooth sequence and without environmental crutches, thus displaying the characteristics of expert behavior.

Experimental Hypotheses About Educational Techniques for Building Response Chains

It is important to distinguish between the order in which responses in a chain are best learned and the order in which they occur after learning. As indicated, these orders may be exactly opposite. Since it is rare for anyone to recite the alphabet in any way other than from A through Z, the alphabet is not usually taught in any other order. However, analysis of the laboratory rat's behavior in performing the chain of responses might suggest an instructional procedure exactly opposite to that typically used. For example, perhaps the best way to teach a child the alphabet would be to begin with the letter Z. This requires nothing but an echoic (imitative) response from the child. Having said the response Z, the child may then be encouraged or given whatever reinforcers are available and asked to say the letters Y, Z, then X, Y, Z, and so forth. (Or if adding only one letter at a time is too boring for a child, it might be better to add two or three letters at a time; "Say XYZ," then, "Say UVWXYZ," followed by "Say RSTUVWXYZ" and so forth.) If the task were to memorize Lincoln's Gettysburg Address, the instructor could proceed by having the student say "can long endure." The next step might be to have him say, "so conceived and so dedicated can long endure," and so on. The process might *end* with establishing the *first* set of responses in the recitation: "Fourscore and seven years ago." At this time, however, these examples are still provocative sources for research and development. The reader is urged not to take them too literally.

Indeed, even if the implications of "backward" chaining proved to be feasible, the weight of common practice in teaching various skilled behaviors works against any tendency to teach these behaviors in a sequence other than those with which instructors are familiar. However, it may be that many behaviors are naturally learned this backward chaining way. For example, a child learns very early in life to wear clothing and even to enjoy getting dressed up for special occasions. Later and very gradually the child learns the behaviors which lead up to being dressed— putting on and tying shoes, buttoning a shirt or dress, etc. The situation is similar with the child's eating habits; getting food into the mouth is the basic initial response upon which is built a whole repertoire of table manners and eating customs. As the child grows older, backward chaining may not necessarily preclude making the material to be learned meaningful to the learner. In the example of learning the Gettysburg Address used above, the memorization process might be facilitated if the learner first read the material and discussed it with others. "Understanding" is usually taught in this fashion. But understanding the Gettysburg Address involves a different set of responses from those necessary to recite it. Backward chaining, in this example, is called for only after initial familiarization with the material. Such prior exposure may give the learner the advantage of strong cues provided by grammar and the logical development of the material. The extent to which the imposition of backward learning upon the prior forward familiarization will set up competing types of responses is a matter for experimentation.

The traditional means of chaining employed in the classroom requires, paradoxically, that some extinction occur as each new step in the chain is added. Perhaps the reason this traditional method of teaching behavioral sequences works is that relearning occurs much faster than original learning. In the usual sequential learning situation, all preceding members of a sequence must be at least partially extinguished as a new response is added, since reinforcement is withheld until the new functional unit occurs (until the new unit which will terminate in reinforcement is formed). The entire process is then quickly relearned with a new terminal response. When a child is taught to say A, then A, B, then A, B, C, he is being subjected to a reinforcement contingency that requires a constant change of the functional response unit. After having been reinforced for saying A, the A response alone is extinguished so it can be replaced with the response unit, A, B, which is likewise extinguished and replaced with A, B, C. On the other hand, if the child begins to learn the alphabet from Z first, from that time on he will (in the ideal case) always be reinforced for what he has previously learned. In backward chaining of the alphabet, Z is never completely extinguished, but is placed under the discriminative control of the letter Y. In other words, it is possible for the learner to be reinforced when he has emitted some other behavior, in this case Y. Y in turn is placed under the guidance of the discriminative stimulus X. In this way backward chaining may prevent the disruption of previously learned responses, since continuous discrimination training occurs rather than intermittent extinction.

Backward chaining may also have the advantage of forcing repeated practice of the final members of a response sequence. In fact, the later a response occurs in the sequence of responses, the more it has been practiced before the entire sequence is learned. In backward chaining the newest elements, those which have been most recently added and are the weakest, are those which are most strongly and recently prompted by the teacher. Thus, the chances of running off the entire chain at each repetition are extremely good. If the teacher has reached M in the alphabet, he will prompt the child by saying "Now say *L, M, N*." The new response L is strongly prompted and quickly added to the chain which now may be run off by virtue of prior practice and reinforcement.

The notion of backward chaining hypothesizes a radical departure from standard educational techniques and requires the use of somewhat artificial situations and responses in order to arrive at the terminal behavior. Perhaps in no other instance of the possible application of learning principles to training technology does common sense seem more challenged than in the method of response chaining. However, demonstrably efficient learning practices may not necessarily be consistent either with traditional practice or with intuition.

The Nature of Reinforcement in Chained Behavior

According to one recent theoretical analysis of reinforcing stimuli, the particular event that constitutes a reinforcement is not a stimulus external to the learner so much as it is the *behavior* produced by the stimulus (Premack, 1959). For example, it may not be food, but eating, that reinforces a hungry person. Thus reinforcers may be defined either in terms of behavior or in terms of stimuli. Either definition may serve a particular purpose, and both are useful ways of thinking about the effects of reinforcement.

Regardless of theoretical considerations, the analysis of reinforcement as response rather than as stimulus makes sense with respect to human behavior. It is often not so much the achievement of a goal that seems to reward individuals, as it is the behavior produced by obtaining the goal. Perhaps the reason that some programming seems to increase motivation for working through an instructional sequence is that through programming it is possible to make one behavior contingent upon another. Instructional material which is not programmed may permit a student to proceed regardless of the nature of his responses to each step in learning.

In any chain of behaviors, the terminal response (the response to the reinforcer) is reinforcing and thus by definition a high-strength response, that is, the probability of its occurrence to the reinforcing stimulus is high. The reason that response chaining works, according to the foregoing analysis of reinforcement, is not that each response produces a rewarding stimulus, but that each response in the chain permits or sets the occasion for a subsequent high-strength response. Moreover, whenever a high-probability response is dependent upon the occurrence of a lower-probability response, the probability is that the weak response will increase and approximate the strength of the high-strength response which is dependent upon it.

The net result of these considerations is that it is the *response* to the reinforcing stimulus, not the reinforcing stimulus itself, that is effective in increasing the strength of behavior to be learned. This analysis would indicate that, in a programmed learning sequence, a student is reinforced not by being told that he is right, but by being permitted to engage in another activity. Thus it would seem that the programmer should use as many devices as possible to permit the student to "go on" through the program. What practical difference this analysis of reinforcing events may make in the future of programmed learning remains to be explored.

Motivational Uses of Terminal Behavior

If responding is reinforcing in itself, it follows that the maximally reinforcing response in a learning situation is the performance of the entire integrated chain of behaviors which is the goal of instruction, i.e., the terminal behavior. The reinforcing properties of terminal behavior may be useful early in training to reinforce student interest or to enhance motivation. Flying an airplane, for example, consists of many subchains which must be acquired by the student and which together form a gross sequence from takeoff to landing. Often flight instructors make a point of letting the student pilot "fly" the airplane by himself the first time up. Objectively, this is not a very significant accomplishment since the plane will fly itself if properly trimmed. For the student, however, it is the terminal behavior which he had thought he would be able to engage in only after long, hard study. Being able to "fly the plane" only a few minutes after instruction has begun can be highly motivating and can provide a basis on which other less dramatic behaviors may be built. After the initial flying experience, the student's feelings of excitement and accomplishment are likely to generalize to other components of the instructional program, such as map reading, weather, fuel economy, and aerodynamics. Other possibilities for using terminal behavior at the *beginning* of training are abundant, and such a training procedure may make a significant difference in the student's motivation.

In many instances, engaging in the terminal behavior of a task at the early stages of training may be too difficult or too dangerous. In such cases it may be necessary to select only a part of the terminal behavior for initial use. For example, no beginning typist can type 60 words per minute unless it is the same word typed over and over. However, retyping the same word at the same rate at which an expert types many words may seem to be a significant accomplishment to a beginner. Often it is necessary to provide the learner with strong external stimulus support, as when a baby who is learning to walk pushes a wheeled toy ahead of him for support. Of all those concerned with the learning process, it will be the learner himself who is most anxious to be rid of such supports when the training program later shows him how it is possible to get along without them.

The reinforcing properties of terminal behavior should not be promised to the beginner; they should, if possible, be given to him immediately and should be used in the technical sense of a reinforcing event. The foregoing considerations suggest that terminal behavior or some form of it might be included at the beginning of a program or program subunit and that preterminal behavior might be programmed to follow it and lead to its "real" performance.

The reader is again cautioned that these recommendations regarding the initial use of terminal behavior are extrapolations from learning theory which require practical development. In attempting to be explicit, the authors take the risk of being wrong on a number of points. However, introducing aspects of terminal behavior early in an instructional program seems logical and the subject lends itself to research. When terminal repertoires are introduced as reinforcers early in training and are supported at least in part by artificial means, it is necessary to weigh the motivations arising from them against the costs and difficulties involved. It is also true that artificially produced early terminal behavior may give the learner a false sense of accomplishment, but this should not be a serious objection if the program follows through with the teaching of real accomplishment. At the present time and in the light of evidence from available research, the foregoing recommendations seem generally sound; in some situations they should be applied with caution, in others with imagination.

SUMMARY

This chapter has discussed the ways in which previously neutral stimuli become the stimuli which set the occasion for particular behavior. Stimulus control refers to the fact that a given subject-matter stimulus, as a result of learning, will consistently elicit a specific response class. Such control requires discriminative behavior—the individual must be able to discriminate or select from other stimuli the stimulus to which he responds. A discriminative (or control) stimulus sets the occasion for a response because the response is reinforced in the presence of that stimulus and extinguished in the presence of other stimuli.

Stimulus control of behavior is established or modified by judiciously reinforcing or withholding reinforcement. A discrimination can be sharpened by extinguishing responses made to stimuli similar to the control stimulus. Conversely, control can be extended to a broader range of stimuli by closely pairing new stimuli with the control stimulus and reinforcing responses to the new stimuli. Various discriminations can be integrated and consolidated by establishing a new controlling stimulus which subsumes them. All these operations vary, for the most part, only in the conditions which result in reinforcement, but they lead to a great complexity of behavior and appear to be basic in designing instructional procedures.

Just as some responses are determined by stimuli in the external environment, many responses are under the control of internal stimuli. The term differentiation is used to describe the increasing precision of responses to internal stimuli. Differentiations, like discriminations, can be taught gradually through approximations, but in differentiation training the way in which a response is executed determines whether it is reinforced.

A major characteristic of an expert is that he is able to perform largely on the basis of internal stimuli and, hence, produce self-sustaining chains of behavior. In such behavioral chains each stimulus serves as the reinforcer for the preceding response as well as the stimulus for the subsequent response. Traditionally, chains of verbal behavior have been taught in the order in which the chain is performed. In contrast, behavioral chains in the laboratory are formed in a backward order from the reinforcing event at the end of the chain. Thus the order in which they are established and the order in which they are performed are exactly opposite. This backward-chaining procedure has possible implications for improving the teaching of human verbal behavior.

It has been suggested that it is the performance of a response that is reinforcing rather than the reinforcing stimulus. Thus, in a sequence of behaviors, the ability to perform a response serves as a reinforcer for the behaviors that occur prior to it. This notion can be used to enhance the beginning student's motivation by allowing him to perform the terminal behavior, or some segment of it, early in training. The early performance of some part of the terminal behavior can provide the motivation for learning the behavior which leads up to final attainment.

REFERENCES

Gilbert, T. F. Mathetics: the technology of education. *J. Mathetics,* 1962(a), 1 (1), 7–73.

Gilbert, T. F. Mathetics: II. the design of teaching exercises. *J. Mathetics,* 1962(b), 1 (2), 7–56.

Holland, J. G., and B. F. Skinner. *The analysis of behavior.* New York: McGraw-Hill, 1961.

Homme, L. E., and D. J. Klaus. *Laboratory studies in the analysis of behavior.* Albuquerque: Teaching Machines, Inc., 1961.

Keller, F. S., and W. N. Schoenfeld. *Principles of psychology.* New York: Appleton-Century-Crofts, 1950.

Premack, D. Toward empirical behavior laws: I. positive reinforcement. *Psychol. Rev.,* 1959, **66,** 219–233.

Skinner, B. F. *Science and human behavior.* New York: Macmillan, 1953.

CHAPTER FOUR

Analysis of Instructional Objectives and Subject Matter Units

The initial problem that arises in starting to build a programmed learning sequence is the analysis and specification of the subject matter behavior to be covered. Before programming can begin, the subject matter must be analyzed into units that can provide the frames or building blocks of the instructional program. The construction of a particular program sequence is determined by both the structure of the subject matter and by the instructional procedures which best facilitate the achievement of behavioral goals such as retention or transfer. In any instructional situation, the objectives of instruction must be defined in terms of terminal student performance in order to permit selection of the most effective instructional methods and materials, the specific subject matter to be taught, and the appropriate instruments for measuring attainment of instructional goals.

Formal procedures for analyzing subject-matter knowledge and skills and for organizing the results of such analyses in order to facilitate program construction are still at a crude stage of development. Generally, programming groups employ nothing more systematic than a detailed subject-matter outline as a basis for generating sequences of frames. More rigorous techniques should be developed in the course of continued experience in the field. Some current attempts in this direction are described in this chapter.

DEFINING OBJECTIVES FOR PROGRAMMED MATERIALS

Confronted with the task of constructing a programmed instructional sequence, the programmer needs to know the performance he wishes the student to attain. Several beginning systems have been developed to determine performance objectives and to provide some means for translating these objectives into actual program-construction procedures. These systems are concerned with both the subject matter to be taught and the learning principles involved in teaching the subject matter most efficiently.

A General Procedure*

The specification of objectives for programmed instruction must be made in terms of behavioral end products, that is, in terms of what the student must be able to *do*—the operations he must be able to perform, the words he will be able to spell, the algebraic equations he will be able to solve—when he has completed a program. If appropriate evaluation instruments are to be selected to measure the attainment of goals, it is necessary that objectives be stated in terms of measurable goals. Carefully constructed proficiency tests based upon the specifications for instructional objectives are essential in developing and evaluating programmed instruction.

The actual written specifications of the objectives of an instructional sequence can be defined as "an intent communicated by a statement describing a proposed change in a learner" (Mager, 1962, p. 3). Such a statement should convey to the reader the specific aims of the sequence. An objective is meaningful only to the extent that it succeeds in indicating the goals of instruction exactly as they were conceived by the instructor or course designer. It should be clear enough so that another teacher or programmer could teach for and attain the same objective.

A specification of instructional objectives should rule out all possible alternatives to the goal. That is, it should be stated in unequivocal terms that are not open to misunderstanding. To say that at the end of instruction a student must know French, or appreciate music, or understand the mechanics of a television set, permits multiple interpretations. Is he to speak, read, or write French? Is he to play the piano, sing the major scale, or recognize Beethoven's Fifth Symphony? Is he to be able to recognize the parts of a television set from a schematic diagram, replace a burned-out picture tube, or, given a malfunctioning set, be able to locate and correct the trouble? Verbs such as "to know," "to grasp the significance of," or "to enjoy" must be replaced by more definitive statements, such as, "to write," "to solve," "to identify," or "to construct," if objectives of instruction are to be clearly defined.

---

* This section is based upon the book by Mager (1962).

A statement of instructional goals should also indicate the conditions which will be imposed upon the learner when he has attained the desired mastery—what he will be provided with when he performs the desired behavior, what information he will be denied, and under what conditions the task behavior should occur.

The following procedure can be used to delineate instructional objectives in line with these criteria:

(1) As a first step, the programmer must specify *the behavior that is to be accepted as evidence that the learner has achieved the objective.* In order to accomplish this, the statement of objectives should be modified until it answers the question, "What will the learner be doing when he is demonstrating that he has achieved the objective?" If the objective is to solve linear equations, it must be stated without ambiguity that the student will be asked to solve, and not derive, linear equations. If the student should also be able to derive equations, this should be specified as another goal of instruction. When objectives for an entire course are written in meaningful terms, it is likely that they will consume several pages; the more objectives that are included, the more clearly is the intent of the instructor indicated to the reader.

(2) The second step is to outline *the conditions under which the desired behavior can be expected to occur.* To indicate that the student should "be able to compute a correlation coefficient" may be insufficient. What kind of correlations will the student be asked to compute? Is the correct solution all that is important, or will he be asked to follow a specific procedure? With what information and job aids will he be provided: will he be given a list of formulas, or must he work without references to any outside help? Answers to such questions may make a great difference in the content of instruction and the materials of instruction used. Rather than specifying only that the student must "solve problems in algebra," a more complete statement of objectives might read: "Given a linear algebraic equation with one unknown, the learner must be able to solve for the unknown without the aid of references, tables, or calculating devices."

(3) The third step in the specification of objectives is *the determination of an acceptable level of performance.* It is important to state how well the student must perform to achieve acceptable behavior. Acceptable levels of performance can be indicated by specifying a time limit in which the behavior must be performed or a minimum number of correct responses or the percentage or proportion of performance accuracy that will be acceptable. It is to be expected that some students will surpass this

minimum standard. Examples of the specification of performance levels might be: "to maintain a minimum typing speed of 50 words per minute for 5 minutes," "to spell 50 words from the following list of 60 words taught during the course of instruction," or "to correctly perform 90% of the following two-digit summation operations."

When goals are not clearly defined, it is impossible to evaluate a course or a program effectively, and there is no basis for the selection of instructional materials, methods, or course content. Moreover, unless the goals are those of both instructor and student, tests can be unfair, misleading, and inadequate in evaluating the terminal behavior attained. Obviously, testing must be appropriate to the specified behavior. If an instructional sequence is designed to teach a student the parts of the inner ear as drawn on an enlarged black and white diagram, it does not necessarily follow that the student will be able to identify parts of the ear when confronted with a colored, three-dimensional plaster model. With clearly defined objectives, both teacher and student will be able to devote their efforts to relevant activities, and evaluation instruments can be devised to clearly reflect the student's proficiency.

SPECIFYING STEPS AND SEQUENCES IN A PROGRAM

In addition to the general procedure for specifying objectives just described, several systems have been developed to analyze both the terminal objectives and the sequence of steps by which the learner goes through an instructional program. These systems are far from definitive and comprehensive, but rather are initial attempts at systematically organizing subject matter content into a sequence of frames.

The ruleg system (Evans, Glaser, and Homme, 1962). This system provides a means of analyzing a knowledge domain prior to the development of an instructional program. The ruleg system is founded on the premise that the verbal subject matter that appears in a program can be classified into two groups of statements, rules and examples. The rules are called "ru's" and the examples "eg's"; hence the name "ruleg."

Definitions of ru's and eg's are relative; sometimes a rule can be an example and an example can be a rule. In general, a rule is a definition, a mathematical formula, an empirical law, a principle, an axiom, or an operating procedure from any area of knowledge. The main feature of a rule is that it is a statement of some generality for which substitution instances or examples can be obtained. An example is a description of a physical event, a deduction or theorem, or a statement of a relationship between physical or conceptual objects. The main feature of all eg's is that they are statements of some specificity derived from more generalized rules. The clearest examples of rules and their corresponding eg's are in mathematics. The algebraic statement that $a + b = b + a$ is a rule which summarizes an infinite number of substitution instances, one example being $7 + 2 = 2 + 7$. The latter statement is in turn a rule for an example of such a statement as 7 stones + 2 stones = 2 stones + 7 stones. It is also possible that the initial algebraic statement $a + b = b + a$ can be an example of a rule in mathematical theory such as $a \circ b = b \circ a$, in which neither the operator nor the objects are specified. It is not difficult to generate illustrations or ru's and eg's in different subject matter areas. For instance, the statement "Materials which offer a very high resistance to the flow of current are known as insulators" is a rule, an example of which would be "Glass has a high resistance to the flow of current and therefore is an insulator." Or a rule might be "A sonnet is a poem of 14 lines written in iambic pentameter" and the corresponding example " 'Shall I Compare Thee to a Summer's Day' is a sonnet."

The first step in constructing a programmed learning sequence by the ruleg system is the specification of the terminal behavior. The programmer must outline, as precisely as possible, both the responses he wants from the student at the end of the program and the stimuli or clues in the presence of which the student will be expected to make these responses. At this point, questions such as those previously suggested in this chapter must be answered. If the student is studying statistics, will he have to produce a formula on his own, or will he have a book available? Is he being prepared to write a short essay comparing two statistical tests or will he be called upon to take a multiple-choice test at the end of the program? With what stimulus supports may the student provide himself while his criterion behavior is being assessed—another student, the instructor, his notes? The construction and form of the program may differ radically as a function of the criterion behavior chosen.

The second step is to write down all the pertinent subject matter rules. A subject matter expert should try to do this without the external support of texts, manuals, notes, or other references in order to free himself from traditional ways of approaching the subject matter. While the subject-matter expert may be able to think of nearly all the ru's needed for the program, the programmer writing a new course as he learns it himself may need to systematically explore pertinent references for additional ru's. Each ru should be written on a separate index card in order to facilitate re-ordering and arrangement during later steps.

The third step is to arrange the ru index cards in an approximate order for program presentation. The ordering scheme will be different for different subject matters. Ordering may be according to a continuum of complexity (introduction of simpler ru's first), chronology (as in a history program), spatiality (as in a geography program), or dependence upon other ru's. Interdependent relationships among rules should be carefully considered, because the understanding of one rule may depend upon the mastery of some other rules. For example, ru's defining resistance in an electronics program should be introduced before ru's about Ohm's law, since the statement of Ohm's law involves the definition of resistance.

	RU 1	RU 2	RU 3	• • •
RU 1				
RU 2				
RU 3				
• • •				

FIGURE 1. A Rule Matrix.

Step four calls for the construction of a matrix for systematically comparing and interrelating all of the rules. From an instructional point of view, it is this ability to relate rules to one another that is a major aspect of "understanding"; hence a technique of programming which systematically prepares these interrelationships is of great value. A rule matrix is made by listing all of the ru's vertically down a sheet of paper, and also listing them horizontally across the top of the paper, as shown in Fig. 1. Each cell in the matrix represents one possible comparison between ru's, and the matrix permits the ru's of a subject to be systematically examined for similarities, differences, possible confusion, and connections that may exist. The matrix may also lead to comparisons or relationships which have not been previously considered. The upper left corner of the matrix is reserved for the operators which interrelate the ru's. A very general operator such as "relation" might be used whereby each ru would be compared with every other to determine the nature of their relationship, e.g., "How is ru 2 related to ru 1?" Another useful operator might be "discrimination," and ru's would be compared to determine how each ru differs from every other ru. This procedure may facilitate discrimination training when the ru's have certain similarities which can confuse the student. The major diagonal of the matrix relates each rule to itself, and this diagonal is reserved for definition cells. A ru is related to itself by being defined in terms of some previous behavior which the student has and which can be used to make the definition meaningful.

Step five requires the programmer to generate examples (eg's) for each of the ru's and ru relationships in his matrix. It is mainly through eg's that the student will interact with the subject matter. In addition, eg's are useful in providing practice and review for the ru during the process of attaining the terminal objective. A full range of examples must be used if an adequately generalizable rule is to be learned, including simple examples, complex cases, and instances set in unique contexts. A good guideline for the first eg is that it be the simplest possible nontrivial example, leaving more complex examples for later stages in the program.

Step six calls for the programmer to number each cell in the matrix according to a proposed order of presentation. Often the intersection of each rule with itself (definition frames) can be used to start a sequence. Then the remaining cells are examined to determine which ru's are to be included in the program and which are to be omitted.

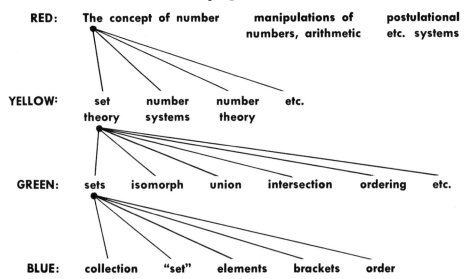

FIGURE 2. An Illustrative Subcategory Breakdown Used in Subdividing Subject Matter Units.

The cells to be used are numbered sequentially, and the numbered ru matrix is used later in assembling the frame sequences in the program. After the cells have been ordered, the programmer can begin to construct frames by judicious selection and combination of the eg's and ru's that have been generated.* An example of the use of the ruleg system in writing a program on basic electricity is to be found in Thomas, Davies, Openshaw, and Bird (1963).

Subdivision of subject matter units. Another suggestion for systematizing the programmer's task is somewhat simpler than the ruleg system (Mechner, 1961). With this procedure the programmer begins by outlining the material to be taught in considerable detail. The outline should begin with 5 to 20 major headings that correspond roughly to the chapter headings of a textbook. The number of headings to be used depends on the scope of the program. Each heading is written on a red index card, and the cards are ordered in some rational sequence. Subheadings under each red card heading are then written on yellow index cards and subsequently ordered. The process of subdivision is continued for two more stages, on green and then blue cards. The words, phrases, and concepts written on the blue cards should be the "atoms" of the subject matter and should be so elementary that a new blue card can be introduced every 5 to 10 frames in a program. That is, of course, an average rate, since several blue concepts might be involved in one frame and some concepts might require more frames than others. To illustrate

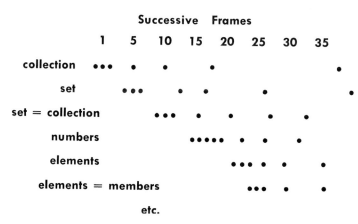

FIGURE 3. A Program Flow Chart.

* Specific frame writing techniques are discussed in Chapters 5 and 6 of this volume, and specific rules for the combination of ru's and eg's are discussed in Evans, Glaser and Homme (1962).

the subdivision process using set theory, the author of this system has given the diagram shown in Fig. 2.

A flow chart is then used to facilitate the introduction and manipulation of the subject matter units. The use of the flow chart centers around the systematic "thinning out" or decreasing coverage of an item after its introduction. For example, three to six consecutive frames deal with the same blue-level item when it is introduced. Thereafter, review of that item is interspersed in decreasing frequency among frames for other items. The flow chart in Fig. 3 shows how the intensity of treatment is gradually diminished following the introduction of a concept. Every dot represents a response to be made by the student. Several dots in the same vertical column indicate that the concepts represented will be integrated in that frame. The illustrative frames given below are for the subject matter described in Figs. 2 and 3.

A collection of dishes can also be called a set of dishes. Several crayons can be called a _____ of crayons.

                                         Response: set

Every member of the set of crayons is called an element of the set. Every member of the set of dishes, similarly, would be called _____.

                                         Response: an element

---

In general, the members of a set are called its _____.

                                         Response: elements

A collection of elements is a _____.

                                         Response: set

Make a sentence using the words **set** and **element**.

                                         Response: A set is defined as a collection of elements.

To systematize the planning of a frame sequence, a special stencil or template may be used which automatically thins out the review of a concept according to a predetermined schedule and varies the rate of review according to the complexity of the concept involved. On the basis of the complexity of the concept, the programmer must estimate what ratios of review frames to teaching frames will be most effective. A difficult concept will require intensive initial treatment and more frequent review; a trivial concept will require minimal initial treatment and less frequent review. Prior to using the stencil, the programmer must decide upon the point at which each new concept will be introduced and the appropriate ratio of review to be used for each concept. The programmer is advised not to adhere rigidly to the pattern indicated by the stencil; the purpose of the device is only to remind the programmer of what must be reviewed and to aid him in the systematic scheduling of review items. Data obtained from student tryout are then used to adjust the extent of necessary review.

Discrimination flow. A third method, which is also at an early stage of development, calls for the subject matter expert and the programmer to identify the sequences of discriminations that are required in order to perform the terminal behavior (Evans, 1961; Glaser, 1963; Homme, 1961). The specified flow of response units to be taught is set out in a flow chart like the mathematics example shown in Fig. 4. The diamond-shaped

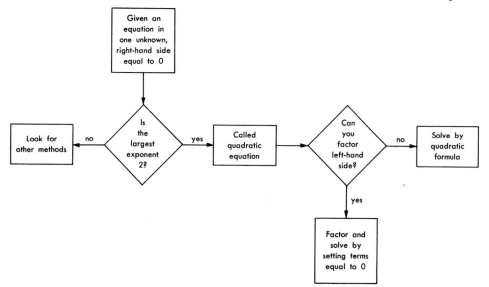

FIGURE 4. A Flow Chart in Mathematics.

boxes contain questions or frame-content on the basis of which a discrimination is made, and the rectangles are the appropriate discriminative responses. Beginning with the problem in the upper box, a discrimination must be made as to whether the largest exponent is 2. If the largest exponent is not 2, the quadratic method of solution cannot be used. If it is 2, the correct discriminative response is that the expression is called a quadratic equation. The next discrimination involves deciding whether the equation can properly be factored. If the answer is "no," the problem is solved in one way; if the answer is "yes," a different kind of behavior is appropriate. Such a flow chart is made up in conjunction with the subject matter expert and serves as a guide which the programmer can follow and which can be checked by subject matter reviewers. The users of this procedure seem to find that a great deal of behavior can be handled, without too much distortion, in terms of the flow of discriminative responses.

Mathetics. Recently an approach to the construction of teaching exercises similar to programmed sequences has been described under the title of "mathetics" (Gilbert, 1962a; Gilbert, 1962b). Mathetics is defined as the systematic application of reinforcement theory to the analysis and construction of complex repertoires which represent mastery of subject matter. The system is rather technical. In it behavior is considered in terms similar to those described in Chapters 2 and 3 of this volume. Behavior is generally classified as involving discrimination, generalization, and chaining, and the strategy of an instructional sequence is varied as necessary to teach for these three behavioral classes. The unit in a mathetical sequence is called an "exercise" in order to distinguish it from the usual "frame" in programmed instruction. Little restriction is put on the size or extent of an exercise. Its size is determined not by "breaking the material into small parts," but by determining how big a step a student can reasonably take at the moment. In order to determine what courses of instruction might interfere with or facilitate learning, detailed analysis is also made of the behavior of the student and the responses indicated by the subject matter. As in the discrimination flow procedure previously described, analysis is made of the discriminations and generalizations required for mastery of subject matter. The mathetical technique discusses procedures for analyzing the terminal behavior to be taught and for planning the sequence of instruction. In general, the simple formula of a frame with blank spaces is abandoned in order to keep the performance of the learner as appropriate as possible to the terminal behavior to be mastered.

TASK TAXONOMIES

The crucial problem in analyzing terminal behavior is how to describe instructional objectives in a detailed manner that is meaningful for instruction. Attempts have been made to develop taxonomies or classification schemes for performance objectives. However, at the present time the development of such classifications of behavior requires further elaboration in order that their usefulness may be increased for specifying the objectives of instruction (cf. Gagné and Bolles, 1959; Miller, 1962a; Miller, 1962b).

What the instructional specialist requires for specifying the terminal behavior is a set of descriptive categories which tell him how to proceed, since the conditions of efficient learning are undoubtedly different for different tasks. An analysis by Gagné (1965) is a major attempt along these lines. Gagné formulates behavior categories in which he suggests the conditions for learning the kind of behavior in each classification. Seven categories are considered:

(1) *Response learning.* This is a basic form of learning which is prerequisite to other learning. An example is echoic verbal behavior in which the response is a sound pattern somewhat similar to the stimulus, such as occurs when a child, in the presence of the discriminative stimulus of his father, learns to say "Daddy" to the stimulus supplied by the parent, "Say daddy." Other examples are learning to write the characters of shorthand and learning to make unfamiliar language sounds in foreign language instruction. Involved in this kind of learning is response differentiation, as discussed in earlier chapters. The basic condition required for this kind of learning is contiguity of the response following stimulus; "Say daddy" must be closely followed in time by the response "Daddy." Reinforcement for the learner can be both the response-produced stimuli as the result of making the response and the response of the father.

(2) *Associations.* A stimulus comes to be associated with a response in such a way that in the presence of the stimulus the response occurs with a high probability. A child has acquired an association when he learns a new word in naming an object. Other examples are learning new technical words or new words in a foreign language or learning to push a new button on the dashboard of an unfamiliar automobile. Gagné asserts that association learning involves a three-member chain. First, there must be the discrimination of the S from the surrounding environment; the S must become an S^D. (Sometimes this can be done by verbal instructions

which serve to call out responses which in turn point out the appropriate stimuli.) Second, the differentiated response must be available in the learner's repertoire occasioned by the response learning mentioned above. Third, the existence of previous learning in the student's entering repertoire, not necessarily exhibited in overt behavior, becomes a meaningful or thematic link between the stimulus and the response. Thus, in learning the response "flower" to the word "red," the following chain might be involved:

$$S_{RED} \rule{1cm}{0.4pt} r_{rose} \cdot s_{rose} \rule{1cm}{0.4pt} r_{flower} \cdot s_{flower} \rule{1cm}{0.4pt} R_{FLOWER}$$

The existence of such meaningful associations from the learner's past can provide learning prompts (to be discussed in Chapter 5) which facilitate the instructional process.

In simplest form, the outcome of association learning is that, upon presentation of a stimulus, a response is made which is other than a copying or echoic response. Essentially, the stimulus is named or identified. This behavior can be produced in an instructional situation in which the continuity of the S^D, intervening prompting associations, and the R is brought about.

(3) *Multiple discrimination.* Behavior in this category occurs when the individual makes several different responses to an equal number of stimuli; the individual discriminates or identifies two or more different stimuli, for example, in learning a resistor color code where he learns to associate ten different colors with the numerals 0 through 9; in learning a foreign language vocabulary; and in distinguishing the locations and names of instruments on a panel. Multiple discrimination consists basically of the forming of associations described in category (2) but in the learning of multiple discrimination there is the added complexity of interference, that is, the stimulus associated with one response elicits the response for another. A condition which facilitates the learning of multiple discriminations is making the stimuli as distinctive as possible to minimize interference. Gagné lists some suggestions for making the stimuli of a task more distinctive; this essentially involves the use of prompting. A further learning condition for teaching multiple discrimination behavior is the availability of the responses required, that is, prior training in response differentiation for the responses that are associated with the various stimuli.

Behavior in the multiple discrimination category involves the presentation of two or more potentially confusable stimuli to which an equal number of different responses are made. The learning conditions re-

quired for this kind of behavior are response differentiation, individual
S-R associations, and methods for making the task stimuli as distinctive
as possible.

(4) *Behavior chains.* Somewhat similar to the description in Chapter 3,
the behavior chain in this categorization scheme is conceived as single
associations put together so that they are performed as a sequential procedure or an ordered set of responses. A stimulus is presented to which
the response consists of making a series of two or more responses in a
particular order, for example, computational procedures in arithmetic.
The learning of a behavior chain involves putting together in the pre-
scribed order a set of previously learned S-R associations. To learn the
order of responses, it should be assumed that the responses have already
been individually learned. This requires the learning of the individual
associations and multiple discrimination training to prevent interference.
Also involved is the backward chaining procedure previously described
in Chapter 3.

(5) *Class concepts.* This involves responses to stimuli which differ in
their physical appearance but which elicit similar responses; the response
identifies the stimulus as an instance of a particular class and distinguishes
it from instances belonging to other classes. For example, such classes
include all instances of "chairs," "birds," "spaces," "the tall one," "the
odd one," etc. In instruction, depending upon the knowledge of the
learner, a concept may need to be taught or might be reinstated by instruction, such as an instruction which says "Choose the odd one." As
previously described in Chapter 3, learning a concept takes place by
learning the limits of generalization within classes and appropriate discrimination between classes. Learning of class concepts would require
response learning and the establishment of S-R associations upon which
multiple discrimination and generalization can proceed.

(6) *Principles.* A principle or rule in the simplest case is a chain of
two concepts: "If a then b," where a and b are two concepts—for example, "If a diphthong is composed of i and e, the second letter is pronounced"; "$ab + ac = a(b + c)$"; "If the temperature of water is 212°F,
then boiling occurs"; and "If two integers have the same sign, then they
are summed as whole numbers in the same direction." Behavior in this
category is described by Gagné as follows: "Upon presentation of a situation containing stimuli classifiable as concept a, and instructions to produce concept b, perform the sequence $a \rightarrow b$." For example, the individual responds to instances of the class of "ie" combinations by pronouncing
the response class of the "second letter."

It is assumed that a major precondition for learning principles is that the concepts which make up the principles must be previously acquired. This point is also made by Gilbert (1962a, p. 54). Once the concepts are learned and have a high probability of occurrence, then instruction proceeds to make one concept as a link in a chain the occasion (an S^D) for subsequent concepts in a particular sequential order. The acquisition of principles and rules is perhaps the common form of learning undertaken by programmed instruction.

(7) *Strategies.* Higher order rules can be composed of simple rules. The stimuli that elicit responses involving the application of the rules are novel situations to which various rules must be applied, for example, when an individual has to match a series of stimuli in order to discover what properties they have in common. Such processes (strategies) are involved in making inferences, in classifying observations, etc. Essentially behavior in this category involves discovering the principles applicable to a series of situations that are new to the individual. The learner uses principles, as described in the previous category, in order to discover the principles appropriate to a set of new stimulus situations. Prerequisite to the learning of strategies is appropriate competence in the behavioral categories previously described.

Designing instructional sequences. Viewing the process of instruction in terms of these categories, Gagné emphasizes the following:

1. Designing optimal instruction is a matter of choosing the proper tactics for each of six categories of behavior implied by the formal (non-content) characteristics of instructional objectives (tasks).

2. Any set of instructional objectives may require one or more, or any combination, of these tactics to insure that learning occurs most effectively. An excellent description of this problem and its complexities is given by Gilbert (1962b).

3. For each type of behavior shown, the process of learning in its pure form is exceedingly quick, and depends mainly on the contiguous occurrence of certain stimulus and response events.

4. The impurities in learning, which occasion slowness and difficulty, are largely attributable to insufficient preconditioning of the learner, so that more than one kind of behavior has to be acquired at one and the same time. Since optimal conditions for learning are different for each type, this results in ineffective tactics.

A taxonomy of educational objectives. A taxonomy for a wide range of goals in education has been described by a committee of educational specialists (Bloom, 1954). Educational objectives are classified in three ways. First, a verbal description or definition is presented for each class and subclass. Second, each definition is exemplified by a list of objectives selected from materials describing objectives of the curriculum and of achievement tests. Third, the behavior described in each class definition is further exemplified by illustrations of examination questions and problems which are considered appropriate to each class. The test questions are considered to be the most detailed and precise definition of the class since they show the tasks the student is expected to perform and the specific behavior he is to exhibit. The important emphasis of this approach is the specification of instructional objectives in terms of items on a detailed test of student proficiency.

A SUGGESTED APPROACH

In this section, the attempt is made to present an outline which can be generally useful in analyzing and organizing a subject matter domain in a way that facilitates the development of an instructional program. The steps described are presented to give a general framework within which the program developer can use his own subject matter knowledge, his pedagogical experience, and his knowledge of principles of learning and instruction.

Step 1. Identification of the terminal repertoire. The "terminal repertoire" refers to what is commonly designated as mastery of a given subject matter. An essential task involved in this step is that of analyzing this behavior. As has been indicated earlier in this chapter, it is the specification of the techniques to be used in this analysis, or rather the absence of such techniques, which is a major stumbling block in program construction.

The teacher-programmer usually wants to get on with the teaching task rather than write detailed specifications. However, it seems difficult to program what one might not see in clear detail—at least enough detail to begin, since it is true that the behavior required by the student often becomes clearer in the course of preparing specific instructional procedures. The outline presented here suggests breaking the subject matter into units which are small enough to allow the programming and behavioral specification to proceed together and to permit some interplay between the analysis of terminal behavior and the techniques for teaching that behavior.

This first step calls for an abstract of the terminal behavior, that is, enumeration of what the student can *do* when he has finished the pro-

gram. Events that are unobservable or without specific behavioral reference are to be avoided. When words like "understanding," "reason," and
"have insight" are used, they should refer to some observable examples of
student performance. In this step the listing of a terminal repertoire may
not run to more than a few pages in length and may be as brief as, for
example, "Recite the multiplication tables up to 12," or "Describe the
stages of mitosis." If the subject matter requires that the student learn
many rules, then a specification of the terminal repertoire should include
not only the rules themselves but a statement of what is to be done with
the rules. Are they to be memorized and recited ("What are the laws of
thermal transmission?"), or should the application of these rules be
stressed? The short book by Mager (1962) is a good treatment of how
terminal behavior can be stated and provides many helpful examples. In
addition to specific statements of student behavior, it is also helpful to
write down all technical terms, symbols, abbreviations, and similar special items peculiar to the subject matter. This list of terms can help
insure that no definitions necessary for subject matter mastery are left
unprogrammed.

In a sense, what the programmer is doing in listing the terminal repertoire is suggesting the terminal frames in a short program or in sections
of a long program. The terminal frames should demand that the student
perform the skill described in the abstract of terminal behavior, and the
program sequence is designed to teach this behavior.

The level of analysis and amount of detail required in this step is
difficult to prescribe. Too general a description does not include essential details and too specific a description may be unnecessary and time
consuming. In this first step the description of the terminal repertoire
should reflect a level of analysis which permits the programmer to get on
with the task. An experienced teacher and an expert in the subject matter
should be able to specify an appropriate level.

Step 2. Identifying the student and his entering repertoire. Entering
behavior has been much less discussed in programming literature than
terminal behavior, but it is of no less importance. The behavior the
student brings to the program determines the level at which the program
must start and provides the base upon which the program builds. The
existing competencies of the student must be employed to develop new
subject matter competencies, and the specificity of program construction
requires an explicit statement of his entering behavior. The entering
behavior can then be developed and guided. Program tryout will often
dramatically point out where the programmer has assumed too little or

too much in his target population. Frequently it is the vagueness of the entering behavior requirement which contributes to an apparently ineffective program.

Again a listing of specific skills and knowledges is required. Again a list of the required vocabulary, verbal or symbolic, is a helpful way to proceed; for example, does the student have to know the function of a rheostat? must he know how piston engines work? The safest tack is to assume that the typical student knows somewhat less than his educational history would indicate. While often not done in presently available programs, it is desirable to develop a program pretest which assesses the requirements necessary to enter the program.

Step 3. Formulating criterion achievement measures. Student attainment must be demonstrated and assessed by achievement tests appropriate to the objectives of the program. These criterion measures can be available standardized tests *if* these tests are judged to adequately measure what is taught in the program. If this is not the case, tests appropriate to the program must be developed, and these may be used in conjunction with the more general standardized tests. The most significant characteristic of measures of criterion achievement is that they help to specifically pin down the identification of terminal behavior begun earlier in Step 1. In the construction of the specifications for a detailed achievement test, the programmer will be required to define the context and material environment in which the student must perform: the tools, references, and instruments that the student is permitted to use.

Instructional situations and achievement tests necessarily constitute only samples of the total amount of subject matter. No lesson teaches and no test assesses all possible subject matter instances in which a student will perform, although in teaching addition with single-digit numbers or in teaching a list of spelling words it is possible to come close to testing the universe of content. Even in these cases, however, it is usually hoped that there are certain spelling rules and concepts of addition which are generalizable. Consequently, it is desirable that the program employ an adequate sample of subject matter which gives the student a wide basis for generalization and that the achievement tests then give the student another sample of subject matter in which the student demonstrates his mastery and the extent to which he has learned generalizable behavior. This procedure helps get around the criticism of "teaching for the test." In addition, it appears necessary to experimentally determine the kind of subject matter in the program which maximizes the ability to generalize.

Experienced test constructors, in working with the programmer and with the stated objectives of the program, can provide an important contribution in this phase and can take over the task of test construction. The completed test can be used as a document which describes in detail the coverage of terminal behavior stated generally in Step 1. The test is used both to assess student attainment and to assess the adequacy of the program in the course of its development. Step 3, then, extends the original statement of terminal behavior by examining relevant criterion measures (the terminal environments in which the student must perform) and sets up the specifications for the development of appropriate criterion achievement tests.

Step 4. Specification of content subtopics and component repertoires. A subject matter expert can generally divide his subject into subtopics primarily on the basis of content interrelationships and the logic and structure of the subject matter. In contrast, a psychologist should consider subject matter analysis in less content-oriented terms and more in terms of the behavior of the learner and the kind of stimulus-response situations involved. "Subtopic" can be used to refer to subject-matter-oriented analysis and "component repertoire" to a behavioral analysis. The concern of psychologists with task taxonomy, indicated earlier in this chapter, reflects initial attempts to develop schemes for describing and analyzing component repertoires. Chapters 2 and 3 of this book also attempt to provide definitions for the analysis of behavior in terms such as discrimination, differentiation, generalization, etc.

A consistent, explicit, and well-tried procedure for analyzing subject matter in terms of its behavioral characteristics is, as has been pointed out, a persistent problem. From the point of view of programming and instruction, the practical requirement is to identify the kind of behavior involved so that the learner can be provided with the instructional procedures and environmental conditions which best facilitate the learning of that particular kind of behavior. The development of various kinds of terminal repertoires requires different kinds of teaching procedures. As more is learned about learning and instructional processes, appropriate instructional procedures can be more uniquely identified with different characteristics of student performances. In the absence of behavioral analyses of subject matter tasks, psychologists working with experts in the subject matter can provide some of this analysis of component repertoire along with the expert's topical analysis; both of these appear to be necessary for the development of instructional sequences. Indication of the nature of the behavioral analysis of tasks is given in the categories presented by Gagné and described earlier in this chapter. Examples with specific illustrations of behavioral analyses in programming science topics are given by Mechner (1965). This paper gives examples of instructional sequences developed to teach terms and definitions, the induction of an empirical law, and the formation of abstract concepts. Other interesting examples are given by Gilbert (1962a; 1962b).

In preparing the component repertoire and content specifications, the program developer can refer to the more general analyses prepared in the previous steps. The kinds of component repertoires will vary with different subject matters and with different complexity levels of the desired terminal repertoire. The main emphasis in this step is the consideration of not only subject matter properties but also behavioral properties of the content to be programmed. At times it is likely that behavioral analysis will suggest a different topical arrangement or pedagogical sequence from that in conventional instruction. If this is so, some experimental tests are called for, and as the program construction and such tryout proceed, new analyses of the instructional procedure may be suggested.

It is also important to point out that the analysis of component repertoires should not be restricted solely to subject matter "discipline." Discipline as used here refers to precision and competence in dealing with the subject matter—behavior that occurs according to subject matter rules. Sight should not be lost of the necessity for giving the learner the kind of interaction with the subject matter which fosters intuition, inquiry, playfulness, and learning from trial and error.

Step 5. Specification of subject matter relationships. As has been indicated earlier, a distinguishing characteristic of a subject matter expert is the facility with which he can generate relationships between various subject matter aspects. Step 5 is concerned with an identification of interrelationships which need to be taught at the end of the program. In teaching a course in statistics, for example, it is desirable to teach relationships between various statistical techniques and show the underlying mathematical similarities. To some extent the necessity for specifying interrelationships is a function of instructional organization and the organization inherent in the subject matter; early in the course, elements may be taught which require later integration; on the other hand, general theorems or principles may be taught early in the course from which the elements are deduced or generated.

Certainly all possible relationships between subject matter topics will not be exhausted. It seems reasonable, however, to examine subject matter topics in some systematic way, for example, the ruleg matrix. Different interrelationships can be considered, such as overlap, similarities, important differences, abstractions, etc., which should be emphasized in instruction. Other relationships are those which a student discovers for himself in a program which has been designed with this skill in view. Still other relationships may be incorporated in criterion frames as tests of generalization and of ability to apply what has been learned. This phase in program development suggests essentially that the sequence of component repertoires and subtopics be examined for significant inter-relationships between subject matter areas and that specifications be incorporated into the program plan for giving explicit instructions in such relationships when it seems advisable.

Step 6. Sequencing component repertoires for instruction. Having specified the component repertoires and subtopics, it is necessary now to plan a first ordering of these components into an instructional sequence. As has been indicated, this is based upon consideration of both the logic of subject matter topics and the interrelationships of component reper-toires. A criterion to be used is of course the sequential dependencies involved in learning subject matter units and their component behaviors. The behavior that the student exhibits when he enters each unit should be clear, whether it depends upon behavior learned in the program or elsewhere.

The entire area of instructional sequencing and learning hierarchies is subject to experimental study, and a significant research effort in educational psychology and learning should be directed toward identification of the properties of learning sequences. Some initial starts have been made as indicated earlier in this chapter. The reader is particularly referred to the work of Gagné (1962) on knowledge hierarchies, the paper by Kersh (1965), and the elaboration of the ruleg system carried out by the Royal Air Force School of Education (Thomas et al, 1963). The end product of this step is to organize the component repertoires and sub-topics in an initial, tentative instructional sequence.

Step 7. Writing terminal frames. After the programmer has specified the coverage and sequence of the material to be taught, in this step it is suggested that he write the terminal frames for each program unit or subtopic. These terminal frames are situations in which the learner will demonstrate mastery within the program. They are criterion frames, for example: Find the square root of 347. What are the common causes of "snow" on a television picture tube? State the results and implications of Galileo's experiment with falling bodies. Diagnose the following symptom, etc. Depending upon the length of the instructional course, the programmer may wish to do this for one part of the program at a time or for the entire program so that the terminal frames can serve to keep the total picture in view.

Accomplishment of the above steps puts the programmer in a position to begin writing program frames. He is free to begin at the point where the learner will begin, or he may work backward through the program starting with the complex units first. He may prefer to try to program units which are very different so that he may get a feeling for the kinds of programming and for the materials required for various parts of the program. The major advantage of starting at the beginning is that a student can be kept working through the program and can provide the necessary feedback for program development.

SUMMARY

This chapter has emphasized the necessity for and the problems involved in analyzing subject matter behavior prior to program construction.

The objectives of a program must be outlined in detail prior to its development. This will help determine effective instructional methods and materials, the specific subject matter to be taught, and the appropriate instruments for measuring attainment of instructional goals. There are some general guidelines for the delineation of objectives as well as several embryonic systems for the analysis of objectives in terms which suggest systematic organization of subject matter and result in a plan for the generation of frame sequences. It is necessary to consider subject matter in terms of both its content specifications and its behavioral characteristics.

The following general steps outline a procedure for organizing and analyzing a subject matter domain prior to program development:

1. Identification of the terminal repertoire. This calls for specification of what the student is to be able to do when he has finished the program.

2. Identification of the entering repertoire of the student. This requires the determination of the skills and competencies with which the student begins the program and upon which the instructional sequence can build.

3. Formulation of measures of the achievement of criteria. This step calls for the selection or construction of appropriate tests to measure

terminal behavior and helps to specify further the terminal performance.

4. Specification of content subtopics and component repertoires. Here the programmer identifies subject matter units and their behavioral characteristics so that appropriate learning conditions can be implemented.

5. Specification of subject matter relationships. This step calls for identification of the interrelationships between subject matter units that the program must teach.

6. Sequencing component repertoires for instruction. In this step the component repertoires and subtopics are ordered into a proposed instructional sequence.

7. Writing terminal frames. The programmer writes the criterion frames in which the student will demonstrate mastery. These frames serve to keep the terminal behavior in view as program writing proceeds.

Following such an analysis of instructional objectives and subject matter units, the preparation of frames can begin and program construction can go through the necessary tryouts, analyses, and revisions. These further aspects of frame construction and program analysis are discussed in subsequent chapters.

REFERENCES

Bloom, B. S. (Ed.) *Taxonomy of educational objectives.* New York: Longmans, Green, 1954.

Evans, J. L. Programmers, experts, and the analysis of knowledge. Paper read at Amer. Assn. for the Advancement of Science, December, 1961.

Evans, J. L., R. Glaser, and L. E. Homme. The ruleg system for the construction of programmed verbal learning sequences. *J. Educ. Res.,* 1962, **55**, 513–518.

Gagné, R. M. The acquisition of knowledge. *Psychol. Rev.,* 1962, **69**, 355–365.

Gagné, R. M. The analysis of instructional objectives for the design of instruction. In R. Glaser (Ed.), *Teaching machines and programed learning, II: data and directions.* Washington: National Education Association, 1965.

Gagné, R. M., and R. C. Bolles. A review of factors in learning efficiency. In E. Galanter (Ed.), *Automated teaching: the state of the art.* New York: Wiley, 1959. Pp. 13–53.

Gilbert, T. F. Mathetics: II. the design of teaching exercises. *J. Mathetics,* 1962(a), 1 (2), 7–56.

Gilbert, T. F. Mathetics: the technology of education. *J. Mathetics,* 1962(b), 1 (1), 7–73.

Glaser, R. Research and development issues in programed instruction. In R. T. Filep (Ed.), *Prospectives in programing.* New York: Macmillan, 1963. Pp. 278–309.

Homme, L. E. Teaching machine applications. Paper read at XIV International Congress of Applied Psychology, Copenhagen, August, 1961.

Kersh, B. Y. Programming classroom instruction. In R. Glaser (Ed.), *Teaching machines and programed learning, II: data and directions.* Washington: National Education Association, 1965.

Mager, R. F. *Preparing objectives for programmed instruction.* San Francisco: Fearon, 1962.

Mechner, F. *Programming for automated instruction.* New York: Basic Systems, 1961. (Mimeo)

Mechner, F. Science education and behavioral technology. In R. Glaser (Ed.), *Teaching machines and programed learning, II: data and directions.* Washington: National Education Association, 1965.

Miller, R. B. Analysis and specification of behavior for training. In R. Glaser (Ed.), *Training research and education.* Pittsburgh: University of Pittsburgh Press, 1962(a). Pp. 31–62.

Miller, R. B. Task description and analysis. In R. Gagné (Ed.), *Psychological principles in system development.* New York: Holt, Rinehart and Winston, 1962(b). Pp. 187–228.

Thomas, C. A., J. K. Davies, D. Openshaw, and J. B. Bird. *Programmed learning in perspective.* London: Lamson Technical Products Ltd., 1963.

CHAPTER FIVE

The Frame Unit and Prompting Techniques

THE FRAME UNIT

One of the obvious characteristics of present-day programmed materials is the arrangement of subject matter into relatively small steps, or frames. From the point of view of this text, frame construction is a matter of behavioral guidance and not only a matter of subject matter exposition. Moreover, the purpose of a frame sequence is more than just breaking down the subject matter into small units for easy learning. While it must be assumed that the subject matter can be analyzed into meaningful units, the mere presentation of these units does not guarantee learning. The point has been made earlier that the needs of the learner are clearly different from the needs of a master of the subject matter. Thus techniques for assuring efficient learning sometimes call for presenting material in a form different from the way in which the material will eventually appear when it has become a part of the student's learned behavior.

The major hazard involved in defining a frame as a unit of subject matter is that a frame so defined is apt to be more "teacher-oriented" than "student-oriented." Subject-matter or teacher-oriented frames often tend to be quite lengthy because the programmer's goal in writing such frames is to fully and clearly cover the particular topic. On the other hand, when a frame is considered as a unit of student behavior, the programmer's task becomes that of bringing a significant component of student behavior under appropriate subject matter control so that the behavior occurs in a significant and relevant context. As the student progresses through successive frames, the unit of behavior may be expanded and increased in complexity so that the student will gradually approximate the terminal objectives defined by the subject matter expert. From the point of view of instructional technology, it is much better to work on the establishment, expansion, and linkage of student response than on the exposition of subject matter units. When it is assumed that complex behavior can be mastered by mastering in turn the units which comprise it, and when it is assumed that a frame is best defined as a behavioral unit designed to add to a complex repertoire that is being learned, it then becomes clear that each program frame must have a reason for existence inherent in the behavior that is being built. Consequently, a frame consists of those stimuli necessary to elicit student performance which is a necessary step toward mastery as defined by the analysis of terminal behavior.

In most published programs, frames are, in general, kept brief. In many instances, the stimuli needed for even very complex repertoires are often few in number and are frequently smaller in physical extent than the behaviors which they direct. However, when the behavior required is reflection about and integration of a mass of material, long frames, elaborate problem situations, and books should not be excluded as program units. On the other hand, there are some good reasons for initially keeping the frame unit relatively small. The purpose of the frame is to permit the student to make a response that is some approximation of the terminal behavior, within a sequence that facilitates learning and retention. In supplying the response, the student is reinforced by displaying behavior that was previously weak, infrequent, or inappropriate in his repertoire. Reinforcement, derived either from confirmation or from the behavior itself, increases the chance that when the student is faced with a similar situation in the future, he will again display the desired behavior. The more frequently this basic learning process takes place, the more rapidly the student may approach terminal behavior. When frames are short, even though the subject matter might be quite complex, the active participation of the student is frequent and delays of confirmation or reinforcement are more likely to be minimal. Short frames, but not necessarily simple frames, also help to minimize the student's lack of attention, often associated with textbook reading.

Behavioral Requirements for a Frame

To provide an opportunity for learning to occur, it is necessary that a frame consist of certain essential parts. The primary function of a frame is to stimulate the student to engage in behavior relevant to the total behavior to be learned. The most important part of a frame, then, is the response or responses it evokes. The second important feature of any frame is the stimulus used to guide the student's response. These two aspects of the frame comprise a stimulus-response relationship which

Example 5.1

The scheme or plan a poet uses to arrange the rhymes in a poem is called a _____ scheme.

                    Response: rhyme

---

already exists in the student's repertoire before he encounters the frame. For example, a frame may present two or more familiar stimuli in such a way that the highly probable responses they elicit are combined to produce an unfamiliar response to the stimuli. This new combination of old behaviors may then be reinforced and strengthened. Example 5.1 is an illustration of this type.* Here the verbal responses, rhyme and scheme, are initially highly probable responses to the stimuli in the frame. This frame requires the student to place the two responses together in a novel arrangement, which would otherwise be a somewhat improbable response on the part of the student. Example 5.2 presents another way in which the two components of frame construction, the response and its antecedent stimulus, can be used to produce learning. Again in this frame, two separate and probable responses are combined to form a new response.

Example 5.2

A nut that is shaped like a *wing* is easy to turn with your fingers. The proper name for this type of nut is _____ nut.

                    Response: wing (nut)

These examples also illustrate a third important feature of a frame: the response is evoked in a meaningful context which is often new to the

---

* It is necessary to remind the reader that examples of frames throughout this chapter are devised and selected to illustrate efficiently the points under discussion. A program on poetry may or may not have a use for the apparently simple frame offered as an example. Frames presented out of context and out of a sequence of developing subject matter competence may appear trivial when presented as separate items. In these examples the student response is given with the frame. In practice, of course, the student would not see the correct response until he had completed his answer.

student. (It is hardly likely that two responses would be put together without some good contextual reason except in humor or drill exercises.) The response "rhyme" was evoked in the presence of a novel stimulus; presumably the student did not previously know that the poet may use a scheme to arrange the rhymes in a poem. The frame was designed to attach the response "rhyme" to the idea of a plan or scheme for ordering the rhymes in a poem.

Example 5.3

This matrix is of the order 2 × 4.

1 0 5 4
8 7 9 6

This matrix is of the order ____ × ____.

8 1
7 0
9 5
6 4

Response: 4 × 2

Frames are often designed to produce responses in a context which is novel to the learner. In the future, this context will tend to evoke the behavior again. The previously learned stimuli used to evoke the response are discriminative stimuli (S^D's). The response under the control of the S^D is the discriminative response, R. The stimulus which a frame attempts to attach to the response or make effective in producing the response is a potential discriminative stimulus. A convenient designation for this novel stimulus in a frame is $\bar{S}^D$. These three elements are evident in the frame (Example 5.3). The first line of the frame sets the occasion for the student to behave in a certain way and is an S^D. The second sentence begins the situation, or $\bar{S}^D$, to which the student must make the response (R) "4 × 2." If the programmer found it necessary, he could prompt the response more strongly by adding more S^D's for the response (Example 5.4).

Frames also contain auxiliary material which the author introduces for interest value, clarity, enrichment, or continuity between frames. Such

Example 5.4

This matrix is of the order 2 × 4.

        1   0   5   4
        8   7   9   6

This matrix, which has four rows and two columns, is of the order ____ × ____.

        8   1
        7   0
        9   5
        6   4

                  Response: 4 × 2

---

material is often a necessity in order to keep the program grammatical, interesting, and readable. The inclusion of difficult or dull auxiliary material, however, may serve only to teach the student to skim over the material or to hunt backwards from the response blank until he finds the information needed to complete the blank.

Frame construction, then, consists of combining the following elements to produce a learning step:

1. A stimulus or stimuli (S^D) which serve(s) to elicit or cue the desired response.

2. A stimulus context ($\bar{S}^D$) to which the occurrence of a desired response is to be learned.

3. A response (R) which the student supplies and which adds to or leads to the terminal behavior of the program.

4. Extra material which makes the frame more readable, understandable or interesting; alternatively, material which serves to bring previously learned material "to mind" so that such material will serve to cue a response.

It is not always necessary for every frame to contain all four of the parts listed. A review frame like Example 5.5 might not be designed to establish a new discriminative response and would omit an $\bar{S}^D$. Presumably this frame would be preceded by others which would establish appropriate responses to "K" and "Fe" and would be presented solely to provide the student with review. At other times S^D's could be omitted if the response were cued by previous frames. This is true of the *second* of the two consecutive frames (Example 5.6). The first sentence of the first

Example 5.5

In chemistry the letters K and Fe stand for _____ and

_____ .

                        Response: potassium

                                       iron

Example 5.6

All mammals bear live young. The human bears live young and is a

_____ .

                        Response: mammal

Birds are not _____ .

                        Response: mammals

---

frame cues the response "mammal" even though many different responses such as "warm-blooded" or "mortal" would also be correct. Lifted out of context, the second frame would appear foolish since obviously the category "birds" does not fit many things. Although the second frame contains only an $\bar{S}^D$ and an R, the correct response is strongly prompted by the preceding frame. Within a series of frames, it is often useful to depend upon the student's momentum or upon his response tendency which was previously established by means of such interframe prompting.

Reinforcement at the Frame Level

In the foregoing discussion of a frame, no mention was made of the reinforcement involved. The reinforcer might well be considered an additional part of the frame, since confirmation is generally used as a reinforcer in programming. As Chapter 3 indicated, however, perhaps the most effective reinforcer in a programmed learning sequence is successfully doing things which could not previously be done. Often the much sought after "joy of learning" can be observed when the learning process results in the learner's ability to engage in behaviors which were previously impossible for him to perform. It can be fun to learn to drive or fly a plane, to act like an adult, or to solve complex questions. Poor instructional techniques often manage to remove much of the fun of learning by placing aversive (punishing) consequences upon *not* emitting the desired behavior, while failing to adequately engineer the situation so that the behavior will occur. The purpose of a frame is to let a response occur, and a good series of frames increases the number of desirable behaviors in which the student is able to engage. In many situations this is a more potent reinforcer than immediate confirmation, and the frame writer would be well advised to capitalize on it in a direct fashion. Confirmation at the frame level may have little effect on student motivation except in situations where the student has real doubts about his answer, as in unusually difficult frames.

A GENERAL CLASSIFICATION OF PROMPTS

A discriminative stimulus is, by definition, a stimulus which has come to call out a specified response with a high degree of reliability. In programming, S^D's are used to set the occasion for desirable responses so that, as explained in the previous section, these responses may be attached to new stimuli, chained to other responses, etc. In the course of a program, however, the student is continually learning new responses or response associations. While the behavior is in the process of being learned, it is weak and unreliable, that is, it has a low probability of occurrence in the proper subject matter context. The student's response to a frame may have a low probability of occurring because he has never or infrequently made the response or because the response must occur to new or altered stimulus conditions. A frame cannot alter the nature of a response or the nature of the subject matter stimulus control if it uses only strong, previously learned S^D's. A program would teach very little if only ready responses could be made to established stimuli and it was unnecessary to respond to new material. In order to get the student to respond to new subject matter stimuli, teachers and programs supply the student with learning supports or "prompts" which help to develop low strength behavior. Prompts are used to serve two requirements of a program. First, they serve to minimally guide so that student responses are not overcontrolled to the extent that no thought or effort is required. On the other hand, too little guidance in the direction of subject matter competence must not be provided. Second, they serve to keep the error rate low so that incorrect responses will not provide unnecessary competition during learning. Prompts, in one sense, are S^D's that have been reduced in strength by such procedures as: (1) elimination of significant parts of the

S^D, (2) the use of different and/or less familiar forms of the usual S^D, and (3) placement of the S^D or a portion of it in new contexts. Defined as above, prompts can be both verbal and nonverbal stimuli and can be applicable to verbal and nonverbal responses (motor and perceptual skills). However, as has been indicated, this book concentrates on verbal-symbolic subject matters.

Generally, prompts are classified as being of two major types, formal and thematic (Skinner, 1957). A formal prompt gives, as a stimulus to the student, a part of the response desired. Skinner uses the example of a theater prompter who, speaking from the prompter's box or from the stage wings, supplies the first few words of a forgotten line to the actor on stage. The actor's behavior is successfully prompted if, after hearing the first word or so, he can complete a substantial segment of his speech. Some speakers on television use a "teleprompter" in cases where there has not been time to memorize a speech. However, if the speaker's behavior is under the control of and dependent upon a full text, it is incorrect, from the present point of view, to say that the behavior is prompted. Behavior under the control of a text or under the control of words spoken by others is clearly discriminative behavior, but may not be prompted in the sense that the individual can operate without continued support. The term "formal" comes from the fact that the stimulus supplied has the same form as the response desired, as when the actor speaks the same words which he hears from the prompter. A formal prompt, then, is a part of the desired response offered as a means of getting the full response (which would otherwise be of very low strength) to occur. A formal prompt is used in Example 5.7.*

A thematic prompt, as the name implies, depends on the general properties of the prompting stimulus rather than on its exact form. It

Example 5.7

To reward an organism with food is to **rein**＿＿＿＿ it with food.

Response: reinforce

* The illustrative frames used throughout this chapter have been taken from various locations in several different programs. Without seeing preceding frames, the reader may not be able to answer the example frames correctly. Moreover, since diverse frames have been used to illustrate the types of prompts under discussion, a group of frames should not be considered consecutive unless so indicated by the text.

Example 5.8

Canis familiaris is man's best friend. Canis familiaris is a technical term for the animal called a _____.

                           Response: dog

The Decalogue is another name for the _____ Commandments.

                          Response: ten

When the hot wire glows brightly, we say that it gives off or sends out heat and _____.

                          Response: light

---

operates as a cue because of its theme, meaning, associations, and connotations. In contrast to the formal prompt, the form of the appropriate response to any given thematic prompt differs from that of the prompt itself. The frames in Example 5.8 use thematic prompts (Markle, personal communication; Skinner, 1959; Skinner, 1958). Often it is difficult to distinguish between formal and thematic prompts and both types of prompting may appear together in the same frame. In addition, there are certain ways of manipulating the format of a frame so as to heighten the probability of a response, methods which suggest neither a strict formal nor a thematic classification. Such methods are included in the following discussion, rather arbitrarily, as formal prompts. The basic distinction between formal and thematic, however, should be clear from the foregoing examples.

If most prompts used in programmed instruction were of the formal type, programs would indeed be open to the charge that they teach only by rote memory. That programs can teach "understanding" is often due to the skillful use of thematic prompting. Because the strength of formal prompts can easily be controlled by varying the amount of the response that is "given away," such prompts are useful in calling out responses never before made by the learner, such as technical terms, complex symbols, etc. However, strong formal prompts, if overused, tend to draw attention toward themselves and away from the subject matter. Formal prompts are generally artificial in the subject matter context and furthermore are not the kinds of prompts available in most tests of terminal behavior. As would be expected, formal prompts are most frequently useful early in a program, and thematic prompts are generally more desirable as a program sequence progresses. This, however, is not a fixed rule, and ingenious programmers have constructed programs with very little use of formal devices. Formal prompts are generally easy to devise; however, the purpose of a verbal program most often seems to be that of setting up intraverbal relationships which are observed when one word or set of words provides the occasion for a different word or set of words.

One traditional way to get a student to make a particular response during initial learning is for the teacher to make the response and immediately ask the student to copy the behavior. This is a common means of teaching nonverbal skills such as lathe operations, dancing, mechanical adjustments of all types, drawing, and so forth. To "teach by example" is to make extensive use of a formal prompt. However, as pointed out above, if the full response is displayed as a discriminative stimulus it is not appropriate to say that the behavior is prompted. In such a case the student engages in imitative or echoic behavior. In verbal programming the desired response can often be incorporated in the frame material as an imitative or copying response (Markle, 1962). The student need only copy the important word or symbol. This device is a means of producing behavior for the very first time and is useful when the programmer must introduce a difficult or novel response as a unit. Copying, however, is not a prompted behavior. The control is too strong for the term "prompt" to be used. Copying tends to be overused by many programmers and, used in excess, results in intellectually impoverished and uninteresting programs. See Example 5.9.

The use of only a few types of prompts is characteristic of dull programs; most frequently relied upon in these programs are formal

Example 5.9

A compound word is made up of *two words*. The word **ballroom** is made of two root words, **ball** and **room**, so **ballroom** is a _____ word.

                              Response: compound

---

prompts using parts of words or outright copying. However, numerous prompts are available to the programmer and the purpose of this section is to present a variety of examples and applications. For illustrative purposes, the listing of prompt types has been made somewhat specific, but within the two main classes of prompts there is considerable overlap among types and the categorization is arbitrary. In reading the examples, the reader should remember that a frame is only a piece of a larger program sequence and that the value of a prompting technique is judged by its demonstrated efficacy in helping to establish particular terminal behavior.

Formal and Frame Structure Prompts

Partial response prompts. A part of the desired response offered as a prompt is the classic example of a formal prompt, and an example of this has already been given. Further examples are numerous. Sometimes only the first word of a forgotten poem is enough to cue an entire line or stanza. In verbal guessing games, partial response prompts are often used in the form of hints which give the guesser the first letter or letters of the correct answer. In the same way, a frame which gives the first letter of a desired word eliminates many possible answers and at the same time keeps the frame simple. When the tryout of a program reveals a frame with a high error rate, the introduction of a partial response prompt will often reduce the difficulty level of the frame. Certainly, this prompt should not be used as a substitute for the addition of frames where they are needed or for frames in which the student should respond without the assistance of crutches. One way of using the partial response prompt is illustrated in Example 5.10. It is an intermediate step in a sequence designed to teach the spelling of "manufacture" (Skinner, 1958).

Example 5.10

> Part of the word is like part of the word **manual.** Both parts come from an old word for *hand.* Many things used to be made by hand.
>
> $\_\,\_\,\_\,\_\,$facture
>
> Response: manu(facture)

Rhyming prompts. Prompts of this type provide the student with a word which rhymes with the response. The rhyming prompt is a formal prompt in the same sense that the partial response is: in order to rhyme

Example 5.11

---

9 times 7 and just 1 more, is 8 times 8 or _____.

Response: 64

---

with the desired response it must give away at least part of the formal structure of the response. Like other formal prompts, the rhyming prompts should be used judiciously. See Example 5.11 (Skinner and Holland, 1960).

Literal prompts. Often a single response may occur in the presence of several appropriate stimuli. For example, both the figure "3" and the word "three" evoke the same spoken response, as do both the symbol "$" and the word "dollar." Whenever the student has been taught to respond correctly to one of several stimuli which call for the same response, his previous learning may be used to extend the response to the unlearned stimuli. A child in first grade learns to read Arabic numerals long before he learns to read the number words. Example 5.12, from a series of frames, makes use of this in teaching number words (Taber and Glaser, 1962). These illustrative frames do not comprise a continuous sequence, but would be interspersed among other frames for different number-words. In the course of this sequence, the stimulus to which the student can respond correctly, "12," is gradually removed leaving only the word "twelve." At the beginning of the sequence, the student is asked to "read" the word (a behavior which he actually cannot perform) but is permitted to depend upon the numerals. As the number prompt is removed over a series of frames, the behavior occasioned by the number is transferred to the written word. The name "literal" for this type of prompt refers to the direct interchangeability of stimuli.

The possible uses for this kind of prompt seem quite broad. For example, in teaching electric circuitry symbols, most people would have little trouble reading the word "resistor," which could easily be transferred to the symbol for resistor by a literal prompting procedure. The emphasis in this type of prompting is to get the behavior to occur in the presence of a new stimulus which will come to guide behavior in the future. Literal prompting, like drillwork, tends to be somewhat barren and uninteresting and could be interspersed with other material.

One interesting variation of the literal prompt may be useful in teaching language pronunciation (Csanyi, 1961). An English (previously

Example 5.12

```
                        12
                  12  t w e l v e  12
                        12
```

```
                  12   twelve   12
```

```
                        12
                       twelve
                        12
```

```
                     twelve   12
```

```
                       twelve
```

Example 5.13

	b	c		b
f	r	h		l
(a)	(ea)	(ie)	(o)	(ue)
a	e	i	o	u
t	k	f	l	
h			d	
e				
r				

established) pronunciation is used to cue or prompt the foreign language (to-be-learned) pronunciation. For example, the "a" in Spanish is pronounced like the "a" in "father." The prompting in Example 5.13 approximates the pronunciation of Spanish vowels. The student is first told to read the English words which are written vertically and then to transfer the sound of the vowels in parentheses to the vowels written between the horizontal lines. Thus, the student reads: "father, break, chief, old, blue." He then reads the vowels as in Spanish: "ah, eh, ee, oh, oo," or an approximation thereof. After some practice, the student may be asked to say the vowels in Spanish without prompting. This type of prompting may have the advantage of reducing the extent to which expensive equipment is required for the beginning language student. Its disadvantage in advanced language instruction is that what is learned is only an approximation of native pronunciation, since the transliteration between languages is seldom precise. A problem also exists in presenting sounds which have no English equivalents, like the Spanish *r*.

Frame structure prompts. Frequently the physical arrangement of a frame can be used to prompt the learner's response. The location of the response blank, for example, can serve to prompt the type of response desired and minimize the occurrence of alternative responses. In the following frames, the student has been instructed that a response blank on the left calls for a symbol (an abbreviation), but a blank on the right requires a word. The position of the response blank indicates, then, whether a word or a symbol is the appropriate response. (Example 5.14.)

A prompt of this kind is more like a direction to the student than an actual prompt. However, such directions or physical arrangements do

Example 5.14

Five millimeters would usually be written as:

5 _____.

Response: mm

In the Kelvin scale, zero is approximately equal to $-273°$ C.
The abbreviation C stands for: _____

Response: centigrade

Example 5.15

Chair factories _ _ _ _ _ _ _ _ _ _ _ chairs.

                              Response: manufacture

---

provide the student with cues about the response itself. Another example of a structural prompt is the length of the response line. Some programmers use blanks which match the length of the response word, or indicate the number of letters in the response (Skinner, 1958). In Example 5.15, no part of the desired word is given away; to the extent that length is a formal property of words, the line-length or letter-space prompt is a formal prompt. However, in this frame, there are two major sources of response guidance: (1) the number of letter spaces to be filled in, and (2) the word "factories" in the frame which contains thematic elements.

Like the physical arrangement of the response blank, minor details of typography and format can play a role in prompting the student's response. The frames in Example 5.16 illustrate the way in which the general frame format is effective in cueing the answer. In the first frame, copying is emphasized by placing the response blank directly under the word to be copied. In the second frame, example prompts (to be discussed later) are strengthened by providing a sequence of numbers in the second factor of each multiplication: 5, 6, 7, —; arranging the example multiplications one under the other makes the number sequences more evident. The arrows in the last frame are used to prompt the correct placement of the symbols.

Underlining is another structural detail that may have prompting value. Any word in the body of a frame that is to serve as a prompt for the response may be further emphasized by underlining; in the frame here, it indicates the symbols to be copied. Underlining is also useful to point up important thematic prompts. Underlining should be used discriminately and cautiously, however; too frequent usage may render it valueless as a prompt or encourage students to scan for underlined words without reading.

Simple prompts, such as the frame structure or providing a partial response, often serve to keep frames short and to minimize error rate at the beginning of a learning sequence. As has been indicated, however, formal prompts should be used sparingly since, in contrast to thematic prompts, they do little to enrich the subject matter.

Example 5.16

Greece is a **peninsula** in the Mediterranean Sea.
Florida is a _____ in the Atlantic Ocean.

Response: peninsula

$$5 \times 5 = 25$$
$$5 \times 6 = 30$$
$$5 \times 7 = 35$$
$$5 \times \_ = 40$$

Response: 8

The <u>M</u>ean is the sum ($\sum$) of scores (<u>**X**</u>)
divided by the <u>N</u>umber of scores.

Complete the formula for the mean: $M = $

Response: $M = \dfrac{\sum X}{N}$

Thematic Prompts

The prompts discussed in this section are, for the most part, matters of narrative, meaning, relevance, and connotation. Used skillfully, thematic prompts guide attention to the text and content of the subject matter. The effectiveness of a thematic prompt depends upon associations between various aspects of the student's knowledge and skills. Through such prompts a student is led to interrelate the elements of his behavior in order to extend their meaning and associations to new knowledge. Wise use of thematic prompting can produce rich and interesting learning sequences.

Pictures as thematic prompts. This type of prompt is introduced first because it may be used as either a formal or a thematic cue. A picture may be used to suggest answers, or a label attached to the picture may serve a prompting function. In Example 5.17 a pictorial prompt is used as a thematic cue. On occasion the learner may be asked to reproduce a

Example 5.17

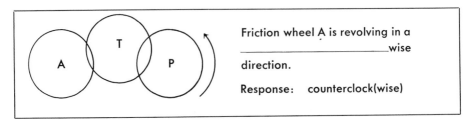

Friction wheel A is revolving in a
_____wise direction.

Response: counterclock(wise)

picture or diagram, for example, in learning to make the symbols used in circuit diagrams. In such cases, the picture serves merely as a copy stimulus or, if the student must complete a partial diagram, as a formal prompt.

Context-setting. When an instructor asks a class, "How is this principle applied in the design of turbine engines?" he is suggesting or setting a context which will evoke student discourse relevant to engine design and not flower arrangement or meteorology. By indicating the topic of conversation, a host of relevant responses assume high strength while other behaviors which are pertinent to other conversations are reduced in immediate strength. In the same way, a frame can be labeled to suggest its context and consequently to limit the range of possible answers. This may be an especially useful procedure when a program covers several topics which must be interrelated or reviewed (Example 5.18).

Example 5.18

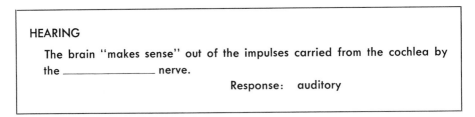

HEARING

The brain "makes sense" out of the impulses carried from the cochlea by the _____ nerve.

Response: auditory

Grammatical structure. If a person begins an utterance with the pronoun "we," he immediately determines the form of the subsequent verb since his audience typically reinforces correct grammar. Similarly, "this" and "these" are likely to be followed by appropriate singular and plural forms. Some languages are more highly inflected than English and presumably grammatical control would be even more effective, as with the French *le* and *la* or the German *die, der,* and *das.* Thus, the grammar used in a frame can restrict the possible answers to that frame. Using a specific article, like "a" or "an" rather than the nonspecific "a(n)" limits the number of responses the student can make without violating customary grammar. Examples 5.19 and 5.20 illustrate the point. The first contains the grammar prompt; the second does not contain it.

Example 5.19, with the grammar prompt:

A candle flame is hot. It is an _____ source of light.

                          Response: incandescent

Example 5.20, without the grammar prompt:

A candle flame is hot. It is a(n) _____ source of light.

                          Response: incandescent

Grammar and also punctuation are doubtfully classified as distinctly thematic prompts. The grammar of a statement is not the same as the theme or meaning of the statement; these are two different aspects of language. However, fitting grammar and punctuation into a formal prompt definition is equally difficult since grammar requires additional thematic control to become effective as a prompt. The two forms of the article used in the frames above obviously, in themselves, do not adequately prompt the response "incandescent."

Synonyms and antonyms. Synonyms and antonyms may be used to limit the response range by prompting like and opposite responses. A frame containing a synonym prompt (Example 5.21) and one containing an antonym prompt (Example 5.22) are given.

Example 5.21, synonym:

Learning usually occurs when an individual's response is promptly rewarded or _____ .

                          Response: reinforced

Example 5.22, antonym:

Reinforcement which consists of presenting sought-after stimuli (e.g., food) is called positive reinforcement; reinforcement which consists of terminating unpleasant stimuli (e.g., loud noises) is called _____ reinforcement.

Response: negative

Just as an antonym may be used to cue a single response word, an entire phrase, statement, or concept is frequently useful in prompting a response which is opposite in meaning (Example 5.23).

Example 5.23

Whereas neural damage in the ascending sensory tracts of the spinal cord will cause sensory deficit, neural damage in the _____ _____ will cause paralysis of the muscles.

Response: descending motor tracts

Prompting with thematic redundancy. It is well known that people use more words to express a notion than a truly efficient use of language would call for. Such thematic redundancy can be very useful as a prompt in verbal programming. An example of this has been described in teaching a second language (Glaser, 1962; Schaefer, 1961; Schaefer, 1963).

Most meaningful sentences contain redundant parts which can be omitted or replaced by nonsense words without a loss in the reader's understanding of the contents. If the "nonsense" words are words in a language currently unknown to the reader, their consistent use should equate them to equivalents in the reader's language. In other terms, the usual redundancy which the student anticipates as a result of knowing English grammar and sentence structure serves as a cue for the responses to be made to the foreign words. Similarly, the grammatical structure of a new language may be acquired to some degree by phrasing the English words according to the grammatical rules of the new language.

The frames given in Example 5.24 illustrate this kind of redundancy prompting at three stages of a program introducing German words. The experimental program consisted of stories by Edgar Allen Poe in which

Example 5.24

Early:

> True!—nervous, very, very dreadfully nervous, *ich* had been, and am; but why will you say that *ich* am mad? The disease had sharpened *meine* senses— not destroyed, not dulled them. Above all was *der* sense of hearing acute. *Ich* heard all the things in *dem* heaven and *der* earth. Harken! *Und* observe how healthily—how calmly *ich* can tell *die* whole story.

Middle:

> *Der* second *und* third day went by *und* yet showed himself *mein* tormentor *nicht.* Again could *ich* as free man breathe. *Das* monster was apparently in great terror run away! Never again would *ich es* see! *Meine* happiness was complete! *Die* guilt *der* black deed disturbed *mich* but little. Some questions were asked *und* readily answered. *Eine* search was even undertaken, but, of course, could *nichts* be found. *Ich* looked *einer* safe future toward.

Late:

> *Die* slope *seiner Wände wurde von Moment zu Moment* smaller, *und der* bottom *der Vortex* seemed *sich* gradually *zu* lift. *Der* sky *war klar, die Winde hatten sich* died, *und der* moon went brightly *im Westen* down, *als ich mich auf dem* surface *des Ozeans* facing *die* coast *von Lofoden* found, exactly *über der* place, *wo der Trichter des Moskoestromes gewesen war.*

German words and word order were gradually introduced. The goal of the program was to equate certain English and German words. Only reading was required as a response to individual frames. The first frame appears early in the program and introduces some key words. The second frame is from the middle of the program and presents the new grammatical structure. Notice that it is possible to make sense out of the passages in spite of the German words and that it seems likely that through continued use of the words in the text the proper meanings will become attached to the new words.

Analogy. Analogies frequently serve to bring together aspects of a subject matter as well as providing strong prompts. The method of using such prompts is often to present one or more complete analogies in the text of a frame followed by an incomplete analogy to which the student responds. These three consecutive frames illustrate how an analogy can be used in interframe prompting as well as within a single frame (Example 5.25).

Example 5.25

It is easy to learn about the Metric System when one thinks of the money system in relation to it. A dollar has _____ cents (pennies).

Response: 100

A dollar has 100 cents. A meter has _____ centimeters.

Response: 100

Thus, a centimeter works somewhat like a cent. Just as 100 cents is 1 dollar, 100 centimeters is _____.

Response: 1 meter

Rules (Evans, Homme, and Glaser, 1962). Response tendencies may be set up in a frame by stating a general subject matter rule. Frequently, such frames present the statement of a rule, followed by an incomplete example of the rule which the student must complete. Rules may also be used to prompt other similar rules. The intention in using a rule as a prompt is not to teach the rule; this may have already been done or may be in process. Rather, the rule is presented as a cueing device, as shown in Example 5.26. The rule prompt frame exemplifies a deductive method of instruction. Often these frames give the student a feeling of accomplishment because he can make deductions from the rule or predict the results of using the rule in particular cases.

Examples. Just as a rule may be used to prompt a response, so an example or particular instance may be used to prompt the completion of a related example or rule. An example used as a prompt may be called an inductive frame, that is, it leads from instance to the general case. In general, a rule may be used to prompt either other rules or examples, while an example may be used to prompt the completion of other examples or the rule which it exemplifies. Some simple example prompts

Example 5.26

> The greatest amount of contrast is presented by complementary colors. Green would stand out best on a _____ background.
>
> Response: red

> $$P = \frac{E^2}{R}$$
>
> How much power, in watts, is being used up by a 50,000 ohm resistor across which 50 volts are applied?
>
> Response: 0.05 (watts)

are given in Example 5.27. By guiding the student to induce a general rule, example frames can also generate a feeling of discovery like that produced by successful deductions on rule frames. The reinforcement the learner receives in having made such inductions and deductions is a valuable contributor to increasing student motivation.

Example 5.27

> During extinction, rats often return to behaviors that were reinforced prior to recent conditioning. Humans, when reinforcement is withheld, may show behavior that has not been reinforced since childhood. Both cases illustrate the principle of _____.
>
> Response: regression

> $$(-5)\,(+10) = -50$$
> $$(+6)\,(-\ 3) = -18$$
>
> The answers to these multiplication problems are negative because _____
>
> _____
>
> _____
>
> Response: A negative number multiplied by a positive number always results in a negative product.

WITHDRAWAL OF PROMPTS

In using prompting devices to cue appropriate student behavior, the programmer is arranging circumstances so that learning can occur. The early frames in a program may result in the establishment of relatively small bits of behavior in response to rather specific prompting stimuli. As the student's knowledge of the subject matter grows during the course of the program, the strength of prompting should be decreased, leaving the student more and more on his own; eventually prompts may be eliminated altogether. Toward the end of the coverage of a particular segment of the subject matter, the programmer should call for increasingly larger units of behavior which the student performs independent of prompts.

Example 5.28
Early:

When two bodies in space tend to move toward each other, we say they
_____ each other.

Response: attract

Middle:

The attraction of two bodies is inversely proportional to the _____ of their distance.

Response: square

Late:

State the gravitational relationship between bodies in space. _____

_____

_____.

Response: The attraction of two bodies
toward each other is directly proportional to their mass and inversely proportional to the square of their distance.

Suppose that the programmer wanted the student to learn the following concept: "The attraction of two bodies towards each other is directly proportional to their mass and inversely proportional to the square of their distance." Such a sentence is only a small part of a total subject matter, and frames concerned with it would probably be scattered among frames dealing with related material. For this single concept, frames taken from early, middle, and late stages of the program might look like those given in Example 5.28. There has been no systematic method presented for specifying the rate at which prompts should be withdrawn. At the present time, the best that can be done is to allow the results of program tryout to suggest what is effective procedure and what must be improved.

The terms "vanishing" and "fading" are often used to refer to the removal of prompts, but prompts may be eliminated in several ways. Increasingly larger amounts of the stimuli which evoke a response may be omitted until only the minimum stimulus remains to evoke a sophisticated response. Prompts may be gradually faded away by being physically reduced in intensity. Still another method is to gradually distort a prompt so that it becomes useless and the student is left increasingly on his own. For instance, prompts may be expanded to a point of nonrecognition, shrunk to illegibility, hidden so that they can be found only with increasing effort, made available to the student upon command, or made contingent upon other behavior. The point in any of these techniques of sequential omission is to eliminate the student's dependence upon elaborate teaching supports so that he can behave as an independently functioning expert.

FURTHER CONSIDERATIONS

The role of prompts. The discussion of prompting strategy presented in this chapter should not leave the programmer overly cautious about the occurrence of student error. The primary reason for keeping error rate down is, of course, to remove the discouragement which follows frequent failure. This may appear to make learning easy, but easy programs do not guarantee learning. A low error rate, produced by clever prompting, is not a sufficient condition for mastery since prompts are a way of getting responses to occur and this, in itself, is only a part of the teaching process. The basic rationale of prompting is not the reduction of errors. Prompts are devices which can help to establish new behavior by assisting in the process of modifying and improving stimulus control.

Program frames must eventually call out behavior which can be given only if the student understands the concepts being taught. Prompts are only a means of arriving at this state of affairs.

Errors and error rate. That student errors are not entirely undesirable has been pointed out by a number of programmers. Parry (1963), for example, has suggested a number of situations in which errors, or no right answers, deliberately encouraged by the programmer, may have desirable effects upon students: (1) Sometimes a student brings misconceptions or incorrect responses to a program and, when this is suspected to be the case, the programmer can encourage the student to make the error in a context in which the error is obviously wrong, silly, or inappropriate. This procedure introduces competing responses and sets the occasion for conditions which can lead to extinction of the undesirable response. (2) There are times when, because of the ambiguous nature of subject matter elements or because of very subtle discriminations which must be made, even an expert is likely to make a mistake. In such cases allowing the students to make the mistake can be used to focus attention upon relevant aspects of the situation. (3) At times a student's interest may be aroused by letting him guess at a response he has not yet learned. (4) The learner can be asked a question to which there is no right answer. For example, he may be asked to express an opinion or viewpoint. (5) The programmer, in diagnosing the entering behavior required for particular sequences employs errors on diagnostic frames to determine whether or not a student is to be sent off on a branching sequence. In view of such considerations, any blanket rule such as "Not more than 10% error rate" is obviously too blind a prescription. Such rules are best forgotten as evidence accumulates and provides a rationale for the planned use of errors.

Determining the response. The programmer must decide what response should be evoked from the student at each stage of the learning process and specifically in each frame. It is entirely possible to write a program which teaches nothing simply by calling for trivial and irrelevant behavior. With respect to the response "blanks" in a frame, the following suggestions can be made: (1) If there is no reason to leave a blank (some frames in most programs present simple instructions or information to the student), then no blank should appear. (2) The response asked of the student should be a demonstrable requirement of the terminal behavior or a means for attaining this goal. This assumes that the terminal behavior has been analyzed in adequate detail. (3) A response should depend upon some significant aspect of the subject matter content: comprehension of a new example, recognition of appropriate subject matter details, etc. (4) A response should be appropriate in extent or complexity to the stage of the student's progress. The maxim that every response should be only a word or two in length is a poor rule to follow blindly. The student should be called upon for the appropriate behavior to demonstrate mastery at each learning stage.

Locating the blank. The question of where, in a frame, to put the blank has been the subject of discussion among programmers. Horn (1963) has argued in favor of placing the blank or blanks as close to the end of the frame as possible since a blank placed early in a frame forces the student to reread parts of the frame. Early blanks may lead to "searching" and disrupt the natural tempo of reading. Horn has also offered the opinion that material placed after a blank is less likely to be learned, especially if it is not essential to the correct response.

A good case can be made for the simplicity of direct questions to the student. Strict adherence to the rule that each frame must include at least one blank often leads to artificial and cumbersome frame structure. Example 5.29 taken from Horn shows a frame written with a blank. The same frame could as well have asked a direct question without damage to the programmer's intentions by asking, "Which triangle has three equal angles and three equal sides?"

Example 5.29

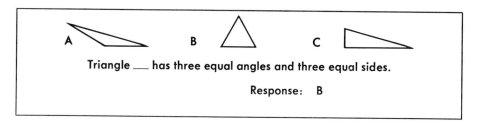

Similarly, multiple-choice frames can serve useful purposes if they are not treated as test items, and good programming helps to make the correct response strong enough to compete with incorrect alternatives. A multiple-choice frame can be especially valuable in discrimination training since it provides an efficient means for allowing the student to compare, contradict, and discriminate plausible alternative responses.

For a recent detailed analysis of research relating to frame characteristics such as error rate and response determination, the reader is referred to Holland (1965).

SUMMARY

The frame is a small segment of subject matter which calls out a unit of student behavior. A frame maximizes the occurrence of learning by permitting the student to respond with some approximation of the terminal behavior in a sequence that facilitates learning and retention. A frame creates a learning situation by combining the following elements: a stimulus, a stimulus context, a response, and auxiliary material. The student's response to a frame is reinforced by the successful performance of the response itself, by confirmation of its correctness, or by the ability to go on to new material.

Early in learning it is usually necessary to arrange for the specific cueing of the student's response since as a learner he is unable to behave appropriately to subject matter stimuli. Prompts are cues which evoke previously learned behavior in the presence of new stimuli, thus permitting the new stimulus-response combination to be reinforced and lead to new learning. Generally a distinction is made between two major types of prompts. Formal prompts cue behavior by virtue of their structure or form. Thematic prompts serve to elicit a response because of their theme or content. Different applications of formal and thematic prompts have been described.

Prompts are useful because they permit the performance and reinforcement of new behavior early in learning and as a result make for efficiency in learning. Formal prompts are probably most effective in the initial stages of a program, whereas thematic prompts are increasingly more useful as the learner begins to gain some competence in the subject matter. As the program proceeds and the student's knowledge of the subject matter increases, prompts should change to suit the student's attainments; the student must be able to respond with increasingly larger and more independent segments of the subject matter. In the final frames of a program, prompts may be eliminated altogether. The withdrawal of prompts decreases the student's need for behaviorial crutches so that he can gradually attain the independent behavior which characterizes knowledge.

REFERENCES

Csanyi, A. P. An investigation of visual versus auditory programming in teaching foreign language pronunciation. In *Investigations of the characteristics of programmed learning sequences.* Pittsburgh: Univ. of Pittsburgh, Programmed Learning Laboratory, 1961. Pp. 135–150.

Evans, J. L., L. E. Homme, and R. Glaser. The Ruleg system for the construction of programmed verbal learning sequences. *J. educ. Res.,* 1962, **55**, 513–518.

Glaser, R. Some research problems in automated instruction: instructional programming and subject matter structure. In J. E. Coulson (Ed.), *Programmed learning and computer-based instruction.* New York: Wiley, 1962. Pp. 67–85.

Holland, J. G. Research on programming variables. In R. Glaser (Ed.), *Teaching machines and programed instruction, II: data and directions.* Washington: National Education Assn., 1965.

Horn, R. E. The rhetoric of programming. *Programed instruction newsletter,* 1963, **2** (6), 4–5.

Markle, Susan M. *Words: a programed course in vocabulary development.* Chicago: Science Research Associates, 1962.

Parry, S. B. To err is human . . . and sometimes desirable. *Programed instruction newsletter,* 1963, **2** (4), 4–5.

Schaefer, H. H. E. A. Poe as a reinforcer. *Psychol. Rep.,* 1961, **8**, 398.

Schaefer, H. H. A vocabulary program using "language redundancy." *J. programed Instr.,* 1963, **2** (3), 9–16.

Skinner, B. F. *Verbal behavior.* New York: Appleton-Century-Crofts, 1957.

Skinner, B. F. The programming of verbal knowledge. In E. Galanter (Ed.), *Automatic teaching: the state of the art.* New York: Wiley, 1959.

Skinner, B. F. Teaching machines. *Science,* 1958, **128,** 969–977. Reprinted in A. A. Lumsdaine and R. Glaser (Eds.), *Teaching machines and programmed learning.* Washington: National Education Assn., 1960. Pp. 137–158.

Skinner, B. F. and J. G. Holland. The use of teaching machines in college instruction. In A. A. Lumsdaine and R. Glaser (Eds.), *Teaching machines and programmed instruction.* Washington: National Education Assn., 1960. Pp. 159–172.

Taber, J. I. and R. Glaser. An exploratory evaluation of a discriminative transfer learning program using literal prompts. *J. educ. Res.,* 1962, **55,** 508–512.

CHAPTER SIX

Frame Sequences and Program Characteristics

The modification of behavior through instruction is usually brought about by many different "learning trials" through the repetition of an increasingly more precise response in appropriate situations. In a program, learning is accomplished by a series of frames in which a response is called for in many different ways. In general, instructional programs can differ in numerous major and minor ways ranging from the arrangement of frames within the program, the use of and dependence upon extra-frame materials, structure and format, response mode, to basic assumptions about how learning proceeds. Characteristics of the program as a whole are probably of more fundamental importance in the learning process than specific frame properties. It is the entire sequence which produces behavioral modifications; the characteristics of single frames contribute to this end.

SPECIAL FRAME SEQUENCES

Different kinds of frame sequences are required in order to modify behavior in different respects. Considered in this way, frame sequences can be classified in terms of the particular behavioral functions they serve. This section provides illustrations of special frame sequences that are useful in program construction and seem to lead to specific behavioral outcomes.

Introductory Frame Sequences

Introductory frames allow the beginning student to respond with some behavior with which he is familiar and thus constitute the first building block in a program. The purpose of an introductory sequence is (a) to acquaint the learner with the manner in which the program is written, (b) to give him some proficiency with the format and display characteristics of the program, and (c) to provide a basis upon which further behavior can be built. Introductory frames should be simple and brief, especially if the students have never worked with a program. Example 6.1 shows initial frames from a program in vocabulary development entitled *Words* (Markle, 1962). Accompanying these frames is a panel to which the student must refer in order to respond:

Example 6.1

Many English words have smaller parts in them. We call these parts **roots, prefixes,** and **suffixes.**
A **prefix** is a meaningful part that is put *in front of* a root.
A **suffix** is a meaningful part that is put *after* a root.
A **root** is a meaningful part too. It may be a word such as TEACH, or it may be a unit that you never see by itself, such as MANU in the word MANUAL.

Read the panel. It tells you what this chapter is about. There are three kinds of parts in many words. They are called **prefixes, suffixes,** and _____s.

Response: roots

The panel says that a meaningful unit called a **suffix** is put *after* a _____.

Response: root

A part of a word can be as small as one letter. The letter -s at the end of a word often means "More than one." The word that means "more than one" is WORD_.

Response: words

As this sequence indicates, introductory frames begin rather quickly to deal with the subject matter and to introduce new subject matter terms which are to be learned. Sometimes introductory frames may describe the program and also give the learner the background information he needs to begin the program. The sequence in Example 6.2 from a basic electricity program lays the groundwork for the subject matter to be covered

Example 6.2

All matter is made of molecules. Wood is made of molecules. Water is made of _____.

Response: molecules

A water molecule is the smallest bit of water that could still be identified as water. The smallest bit of glass that could still be identified as glass, is a glass _____.

Response: molecule

A drop of water could be divided in half and then divided in half again and again. Finally only separate _____ of water would be left.

Response: molecules

Molecules are made of atoms. A water molecule has 3 atoms; 2 hydrogen atoms, and 1 oxygen _____.

Response: atom

---

and in addition places the subject in a particular perspective (*Fundamentals of Electricity*, 1961).

The frames about atoms and molecules are examples of introductory frames which rely quite heavily on copying and not on thematic prompting. The first five frames of a program (Example 6.3) which does not use copying to get the program started (Holland and Skinner, 1961) are provided as further examples of introductory frames.

Example 6.3

A doctor taps your knee (patellar tendon) with a rubber hammer to test your
_____ .

                                Response: reflexes (reflex)

If your reflexes are normal, your leg _____ to the tap on the knee with
a slight kick (the so-called knee jerk).

                                Response: responds (reacts)

In the knee jerk or patellar-tendon reflex, the kick of the leg is the _____
to the tap on the knee.

                                Response: response (reaction)

The stimulating **object** used by the doctor to elicit a knee jerk is a(n)
_____ .

                                Response: hammer (mallet)

The **stimulus** which elicits a knee jerk is the _____ delivered by the so-called
stimulus object or hammer.

                                Response: tap (blow)

Discrimination Sequences

As was previously indicated, much of what the student has to learn in
acquiring knowledge of a subject matter consists of discriminations;
appropriate responses must become established to subject matter stimuli.
For example, to the stimulus, "The astronomical name for the North
Star is . . . ," the student must learn the response, "Polaris." The program
first gets him to respond with the word "Polaris," then he is required to
spell it several times, aided initially by a copy prompt and later by less
obvious thematic prompts. Following this or along with it the program
must equate the terms "North Star" and "Polaris" for the student. In
general, this process involves first establishing a response and then putting
it under the discriminative control of an appropriate context. Sometimes

these operations are best conducted simultaneously and at other times they are best conducted sequentially.

The process of discrimination training goes on continuously during the course of a program and repeated stimulus-response pairings are interspersed with other material in the course of a programmed unit.

Example 6.4

A musical sound has a definite pattern like this:

All sounds can be classified as either music or _____.

                    Response: noise

Noise has no definite pattern to its sound waves.

Sounds which do have a definite pattern are called _____.

                    Response: music (or musical sounds)

If we produce sounds with a definite pattern, we call them _____.

                    Response: music

_____ is sound that has no definite pattern to its waves.

                    Response: noise

A high-pitched sound with no definite pattern is called _____.

                    Response: noise

On particular occasions, however, the programmer may wish to emphasize or give special training in certain important and/or difficult discriminations. To accomplish this, a sequence of frames is constructed to teach the student that a response should occur in one stimulus context and not in another. The frames comprising a discriminative sequence of this kind can occur close together or can be interspersed throughout the program. The short, illustrative discrimination sequence shown in Example 6.4 is from the middle of a program on sound. The response "noise" is to be brought under the control of the stimulus "no definite pattern" and for this reason is elicited in the presence of this stimulus. A series of frames such as this is usually terminated by a frame which combines both control stimuli, that is, noise and music, and calls for a fully discriminated response. Review frames are subsequently seeded in the program to test and to strengthen the discrimination that has been established.

The value of a discrimination sequence is that a learner remembers best what stands out most clearly in the subject matter context, what has been adequately discriminated. A student may forget those associations that he confuses, and forgetting may often be the result of this interference. An individual may be able to remember all of the material in question but not be able to attach what he knows to an appropriate context. The student in such a case lacks discrimination training, not an ability to recall material. Proficient behavior frequently consists largely of the ability to make precise subject matter discriminations.

Generalization Sequences

The term generalization refers to the fact that an individual trained to respond in a certain way to certain stimuli will also tend to respond in this way to similar stimuli. A child who has been taught the label "truck" may also call many other vehicles "trucks." While a discrimination sequence is intended to limit the range of stimuli which will call out certain responses, a generalization sequence represents an attempt to broaden the controlling stimulus range.

Sometimes the entire range of stimuli which should evoke a given response is small enough so that it can be included in the program. For example, the number of different objects which evoke the term "American coin" is quite limited and a program could easily be constructed to cover all examples of American coins. For the most part, however, the programmer does not explore the full range of special cases where a general rule or principle applies. To do so would lead to an impossibly

Example 6.5

Matter is anything which has volume. Water is _____ because it has volume.

              Response: matter

A stone is also matter because it has _____.

              Response: volume

Volume means the amount of space any object occupies. A quart of milk occupies a definite amount of space and thus is a type of _____.

              Response: matter

Some forms of matter are invisible. We cannot see air but it is matter because it has _____.

              Response: volume

---

long program. The word "valve," for example, is an appropriate response to dozens of different objects. Depending upon the objectives of the program, the programmer could cover a narrow or wide range of valve types. He could program a limited class such as "aircraft valves" or "valves used in acid liquid flow." In a broader program, the programmer might teach the characteristics of many different types of valves and then present the definition and usage of valves in general.

A generalization sequence might start and finish with a statement describing the common properties of the stimulus class involved. The programmer should do more than describe such common properties, however; he should arrange the program so that the student will come to state and to use the general concept by himself. Like other types of sequences, generalization frames need not be consecutive and may be placed throughout a series of frames. In the sequence shown in Example 6.5, the concept of "matter" is generalized to several exemplars (Schaefer et al., 1962).

In the sequence in Example 6.6 (Holzman, Schaefer, and Glaser, 1962), previous training about the summation sign (Σ) is generalized to facilitate teaching multiplication (II).

Example 6.6

$\sum_{j=1}^{3} x_j$ means to _____ x_1, x_2, and x_3.

Response: add, or summate

The symbol for multiply is Π (pronounced **pie**).

$\prod_{i=1}^{2} x_i$ means to multiple _____ times _____.

Response: x_1, x_2

$\prod_{j=1}^{4} x_j$ means to _____ x_1, x_2, x_3 and x_4.

Response: multiply

Σ is the Greek letter **sigma** and means to **add** or find the _____.

Response: sum

Π is the Greek letter for pi. **Pi** means to _____, or find the **product**.

Response: multiply

Sigma means s __ __, and Π means p __ __ __ __ __ __.

Response: sum, product

$\prod_{i=1}^{4} x_i = x_1 \cdot$ ___ $\cdot$ ___ $\cdot$ ___.

Response: $x_2 \cdot x_3 \cdot x_4$

The generalization of a response to similar stimuli is an important aspect of learning. A student may be said to understand a rule or concept not when he can recite it, but when he can respond appropriately to examples. Learning to identify and complete instances of a concept often involves extensive discrimination and generalization training.

Chaining Sequences

Skilled or expert behaviors are frequently chains of previously learned responses in which each member of the chain sets up the stimulus context for the following members of the chain. For the beginner, the stimulus context for a given response must be strongly set by the program or instructor. A chaining sequence is a series of frames designed to establish such a complex and self-sustained series of responses. A sequence of chaining frames may start by strengthening individual components of the ultimate chain and end by calling for the student to emit the entire chain.

At the beginning of a verbal chaining sequence, the student engages in a small part of the terminal chain with the aid of many external supports

Example 6.7

1. **Divide 45 by 11**

   Here is what you do:

   a) Since 4 × 11 is 44, the 44 is placed under the dividend ⎯⎯⎯⎯⎯⎯⎯⎯⎯⎯⎯⎯⎯⎯⎯⎯⎯⎯⎯⎯→

   $$\begin{array}{r} 4 \\ 11\overline{)\,45} \\ 44 \end{array}$$

   Now complete the long division:

   b) Subtract 44 from 45 to get the remainder ⎯⎯⎯⎯⎯

2. **Divide 28 by 12**

   Here is what you do:

   a) 12 goes into 28 **2** whole times

   b) Multiply the divisor by the quotient (12 × 2) and put the product under the dividend

   c) Subtract to get the remainder

   $$\begin{array}{r} 2 \\ 12\overline{)\,28} \end{array}$$

3. **Divide 33 by 15**

   a) 15 goes into 33 **2** whole times

   b) Put the 2 in place above the line

   c) Multiply the divisor by the quotient and put the product in its place

   d) Complete the division

   $$15\overline{)\,33}$$

or prompts. As the learner becomes able to supply more and more of the required behavior himself, prompts may be gradually removed. In the case of chains which lead to clearly defined solutions or end products, learning theory suggests that it may be good instructional practice to begin the series with the end product and work in reverse order toward what will eventually be the first step in the sequence (see Chapter 3). The sequence in Example 6.7 shows backward chaining in teaching long division (Gilbert, 1962).

Concept Formation Sequences

As described in Chapter 3, the formation of a concept involves generalization within a class and discrimination between that class and other classes. Example 6.8, taken from Mechner (1965), is such a sequence.

> The first four frames . . . form the concepts of "allergy" and "immunity" by teaching some similarities and some differences between the two. The first frame in the sequence . . . is designed to ensure that one of the very important terms, "antigen-antibody reaction," is present in the doctor's repertoire before the concept formation process is initiated.
>
> The second concept taught in the program is that of "specificity." Note how the term "specificity" is brought under the control of three stimuli:
>
> (a) the word "complementary,"
> (b) the diagram which shows the geometric representation of specificity, and
> (c) the words "will react only with."
>
> Only after the term "specificity" has been brought under the control of these three stimuli is the doctor required to use the term "specificity" as an active response.
>
> In Frames 8 and 9, the new term "sensitization" is introduced. The term is developed conceptually over the next six or seven frames, but note how it is juxtaposed with the previously taught term "specificity" in Frame 9. The purpose of this juxtaposition is to prevent the development of an unintended generalization between the new concept being taught and the one which has just been developed. By an immediate juxtaposition, the discrimination between the two classes is made sharper. This is not only good concept-formation technique, but it is also one of the important devices for enhancing retention.

A good explanation of concept formation sequences is continued in Mechner (1965).

Example 6.8

1

Allergic signs and symptoms occur as a result of the combination of antigen with antibody.

The reaction involved is accordingly called the _____-_____ reaction.

> Complete the sentence above. Then look
> at the correct response to the right ———→

antigen-antibody

2

Antigen A + Person sensitive to antigen A → Antigen-antibody reaction

As the diagram suggests, the exogenous stimulating agent for the antigen-antibody reaction in the ☐ antigen ☐ antibody.

The person provides the ☐ antigen ☐ antibody.

> Place checks in the appropriate boxes.
> Then look at the correct response to the right.

antigen

antibody

3

Reaction of
tissue cells
Antigen-
Antigen A + Person → antibody ——————→ Allergic reaction
reaction

Neutralization
of toxicity
Antigen-
Antigen B + Person → antibody ——————→ Immune reaction
reaction   or infectivity
of antigen

This diagram shows that an antigen-antibody reaction is involved in
☐ allergy only ☐ immunity only ☐ both allergy and immunity.

The antigen-antibody reaction results in neutralization of toxicity or infectivity of antigen in ☐ allergy ☐ immunity.

The antigen-antibody reaction results in reaction of tissue cells in
☐ allergy ☐ immunity.

*both allergy
and immunity*

immunity

allergy

Example 6.8 continued

4

Compare allergy and immunity by checking one or both boxes for each statement below:

Allergy	Immunity		Al-lergy	Immu-nity
☐	☐	Person has antibodies.	☑	☑
☐	☐	Antigen-antibody reaction occurs.	☑	☑
☐	☐	Antigen-antibody reaction occurs on contact with antigen.	☑	☑
☐	☐	Antigen-antibody reaction results in tissue reaction.	☑	☐
☐	☐	Antigen-antibody reaction results in neutralization of toxicity or infectivity of antigen.	☐	☑

5

The geometric forms below depict the relation between antigens and antibodies. (In reality, these substances are complex chemical entities, not geometric forms.)

When we say that an antibody will react only with an antigen specific for it, we mean that their configurations must be ☐ complementary ☐ identical.

Draw the shape of the antibody that is specific for the antigen depicted below:

complementary

6

The term SPECIFICITY refers to the fact that the ☐ antigen ☐ antibody elicited by a particular ☐ antigen ☐ antibody will react only with that ☐ antigen ☐ antibody.

antibody

antigen

antigen

continued

Example 6.8 continued

7

Check the combination(s) of antigen and antibody that would **not** produce an antigen-antibody reaction:

☐   ◯   +   ⊃   ☐

☐   ◯⊣   +   ⊐   ☐

☐   ◯   +   ⊃   ☑

For an antigen-antibody reaction to occur the antibody must be

_____ for the antigen.   *specific*

8

The diagram below depicts the process of sensitization.

Susceptible person **without** antibodies specific for antigen A   +   Antigen A   →   Person **with** antibodies specific for antigen A

When a person acquires specific ☐ antigens ☐ antibodies as the result of contact with ☐ antigen ☐ antibody, he is said to be _____ed.   *antibodies*

antigen

sensitized

9

Some persons are more likely than others to develop allergies. When such a person is exposed to an antigen for the first time, he may develop antibodies to it. These will make him allergic to that antigen.

This process is called _____ .

The antibodies produced as a result of exposure to the antigen are _____ for that antigen.   *sensitization*

specific

Practice Sequences

Retention and breadth of learning can be enhanced with practice which covers variations of basic subject matter rules, operations, and methods. As earlier chapters have indicated, practice which is varied in form and context is a mark of effective programming. Example 6.9, taken from a general science program, illustrates varied forms of practice. The frames of a practice sequence need not be consecutive if the frames are constructed so as not to depend upon close inter-frame prompting. In

Example 6.9

Milli is a prefix meaning _____.
Kilo is a prefix meaning _____.

Response: 0.001 or 1/000
            1000

A kilogram is much (larger/smaller) _____ than a milligram.

Response: larger

A _____ is 0.001 meter.

Response: millimeter (mm)

A _____ is 1000 meters.

Response: kilometer

---

general, most drill sequences would probably be found to be additional sequences in discrimination, generalization, or chaining which are added after the basic discriminations, etc., have been established.

Review Sequences

A review sequence is what the name suggests, a series of frames devoted to repeating essential elements of previously learned material. A single review sequence may consist of any number of frames and may review several topics previously covered. Many programmers, however, prefer to intersperse single review frames throughout the program rather than employ special review sequences. This is often done with decreasing density, that is, review of a particular topic is heavy soon after coverage of that topic and decreases in frequency as the student moves through the program. Such seeding of review is intended to meet the requirements of spaced practice which has often been shown to be effective in studies of verbal learning. On the other hand, it may be argued that review should always be "appropriate," that review should be given when previously learned skills are required for new learning.

In planning a review, allowance must be made for the loss of some of the material due to forgetting or to interference from subsequently learned material. Thus review frames may also have to reteach to some extent. For this reason, it is good practice to start a review sequence at a level of difficulty somewhat below that of the last frames in the series being reviewed.

Terminal Behavior Sequences

Towards the end of a unit of subject matter and towards the end of a program, "expert" or minimally prompted behavior should be required of the learner. This behavior is the goal of the program. Essentially, terminal behavior frames test the teaching potentials of previous frames in a program and give the student an opportunity to perform his newly learned behavior. If the error rate on terminal behavior frames is low, it is assumed that the program teaches. A high error rate on these frames indicates that earlier frames have not successfully taught and need to be revised. These frames are the one exception to the general rule that frames should be revised again and again until they accomplish their goal in teaching. If experts can agree that correct responses to a given set of terminal behavior frames demonstrate subject matter knowledge, these frames should be the objective of the program and should not be subject to revision.

Sequences Using Extra-Frame Materials

Panel sequences. As illustrated at the beginning of this chapter, it is sometimes convenient to use a panel when several frames call for the same illustration or figure. A panel is a separate page or card which the student needs in order to respond to a given series of frames. In an anatomy program, for example, a single panel illustrating a particular muscle group might simplify the programmer's task considerably. Similarly, panels may be used to present a page of a financial journal, an electric circuit, a cell diagram, an organization chart, or a table of data. In general, a panel refers to any extra-frame material to be used in the course of instruction; panels may consist of materials upon which the student can draw or write, which he can take apart, or which he is to assemble. The use of a panel may also add to the interest value of a program in much the same way that pictures in a textbook increase attention and interest.

When panels are used, it is important that the student's responding depend in some way on his having examined the panel. A panel can serve as a reservoir of prompts upon which the programmer may draw. If it is intended that the student learn the interrelationships among parts of an illustration, the frames used in conjunction with the panel should foster the student's active response to such relationships. Such frames may contain directions for using the panel or may simply refer to it, as, "Use Panel 25 in answering the next series of frames," or "See Panel 3."

*Programmed "note taking."** A frequent complaint made by students learning from a program is that the program leaves them with no notes, such as one might take during a lecture, to use for quick review. To permit such review, it has been suggested that responses to selected frames be written on a special, printed note page rather than on an answer sheet or the program itself. The note pages could present a printed summary of the important principles and relationships learned in the program or, depending on the subject matter, might comprise an abbreviated operator's manual. Key words or phrases in the notes would be left blank and filled in by the student as he goes through the programmed material. Appropriate directions would direct the student to place a particular response in a numbered blank on the note page. In this way, the student could construct a systematic outline similar to one he might prepare when studying from a book. A programmed note-taking procedure can serve a useful purpose in showing students how the structure of the subject matter is developed as well as providing a means for review.

TYPES OF PROGRAMS

Programs, like books or teachers, differ in numerous ways. Some programs seem to be direct and matter-of-fact, while others approach new topics with variety and sublety. Such differences among programs are difficult to describe and amount to matters of style and author preference. Other differences between programs are more fundamental and arise primarily from two sources—the nature of the subject matter and different interpretations of how individuals learn most efficiently. This section describes several current types of programs. With further research and development on learning and programming, the relationships between subject matter properties, conditions of learning, and instructional procedures should become more direct, and it should be increasingly easy to construct programs according to specific procedural rules and logical designs.

Linear Programs

The linear program is by now familiar to readers of this manual. In such a program every student pursues a straight course through the program, responding to every frame, with no deviations or reversals.

---

* Stelter, C. J. Personal communication.

Students' responses to a frame are immediately confirmed. Most of the linear programs constructed thus far are of the kind suggested first by Skinner and employ small steps and relatively few responses in a given frame. Linear programs have generally been presented to the student in a programmed textbook or in a teaching machine.

The point has often been made that a linear program is constructed for the average student and as a result may be dull and overly simple for bright students. Eventually, different programs covering the same subject matter may be available for groups with varying levels of readiness, that is, with different aptitudes and educational histories. For the present, good results have been reported when a wide range of students have taken programs constructed for the average student. Good students finish such programs in much less time than poorer students and are ready sooner for more advanced subject matters. This occurs, of course, if the learning situation is flexible enough to permit full use of the self-pacing feature of programmed learning.

Numerous procedures are available, however, for increasing the flexibility of a single linear program in the face of wide individual learner differences. For example, the student might be permitted to skip ahead ten or more frames if he comes up with the answer to a certain key "test" frame, or a high error rate could be used diagnostically to direct the student to a series of supplemental frames. Some other devices by which linear programs might be made more adaptable to individual differences are discussed on the following pages.

Branching Programs

In simple branching programs, a correct response allows the student to proceed directly to the next step of a program while errors sidetrack or "branch" him to supplementary material designed to correct the particular error made. Branching may vary in complexity, and a simple branching program may merely present a short series of supplementary frames and then return the student to the missed frame. With more elaborate forms of branching, whole subprograms might be presented to those students who frequently make mistakes on certain kinds of frames, or each branching cycle might be prepared at several levels of difficulty to permit further branching if necessary.

An advantage of the branching arrangement is that it allows the programmer to capitalize on the diagnostic value of errors. Obviously, a student may make several kinds of errors and the type of error he makes may indicate areas of weakness in past training. With branching, the programmer can supply the appropriate instruction to permit the student to proceed.

Intrinsic programming. The so-called "intrinsic" programs have made the greatest use of the branching technique (Crowder, 1960). These programs consist of relatively long, expository frames with multiple-choice answers. The student first reads a passage and then attempts to answer the multiple-choice question at the bottom of the frame. Each different answer has an associated page number (when the program is in scrambled textbook form) which directs the student to another frame. Incorrect answers branch the student to appropriate remedial sequences. The correct answer directs the student to a page which confirms his answer and presents the next step in the program. An example from an intrinsic branching program follows (Crowder, 1960).

Page 101:

Now, you recall that we had just defined

$$b^0 = 1$$

for any b except where $b = 0$. We had reached this definition by noting that our division rule,

$$\frac{b^m}{b^n} = b^{(m-n)}$$

will give b^0 as a result if we apply it to the case of dividing a number by itself. Thus,

$$\frac{b^3}{b^3} = b^{(3-3)} = b^0$$

but

$$\frac{b^3}{b^3}, \text{ or any number (except 0)},$$

divided by itself equals 1, so we defined $b^0 = 1$.

We used a division process to find a meaning to attach to the exponent 0. Very well, let's see what other interesting results we can get with this division process. Let's apply our division rule to the case of $\frac{b^2}{b^3}$. What result do we get?

ANSWER	PAGE
$\frac{b^2}{b^3} = b^1$	94
$\frac{b^2}{b^3} = b^{(-1)}$	115
The rule won't work in this case	119

The student who elects page 94 will find:

Page 94:

YOUR ANSWER: $\dfrac{b^2}{b^3} = b^1$

Come, come, now. The rule is

$$\frac{b^m}{b^n} = b^{(m-n)}.$$

Now, in the case of

$$\frac{b^2}{b^3},$$

we have $m = 2$ and $n = 3$, so we are going to get

$$\frac{b^2}{b^3} = b^{(2-3)}.$$

So, $2 - 3$ isn't 1, is it? It's -1.

Return to Page 101, now, and quit fighting the problem.

The student who elects page 119 will find:

Page 119:

YOUR ANSWER: The rule won't work in this case.

Courage! The division rule got us through b^0, where $m = n$, and it will get us through the case where m is smaller than n. In this case we have

$$\frac{b^2}{b^3} = ?$$

and applying the rule

$$\frac{b^m}{b^n} = b^{(m-n)}$$

we get

$$\frac{b^2}{b^3} = b^{(2-3)}.$$

So the exponent of our quotient is $(2 - 3)$ which is -1, isn't it? So just write

$$\frac{b^2}{b^3} = b^{(2-3)} = b^{(-1)}$$

as if you knew what it meant.

Now return to Page 101 and choose the right answer.

And the student who chooses the right answer will find:

Page 115:

YOUR ANSWER: $\dfrac{b^2}{b^3} = b^{(-1)}$

You are correct. Using our rule for division

$$\frac{b^m}{b^n} = b^{(m-n)}$$

in the case of

$$\frac{b^2}{b^3}$$

we get

$$\frac{b^2}{b^3} = b^{(2-3)} = b^{(-1)}.$$

Now, by ordinary arithmetic, we can see that

$$\frac{b^2}{b^3} = \frac{b \times b}{b \times b \times b} = \frac{\cancel{b} \times \cancel{b}}{\cancel{b} \times \cancel{b} \times b} = \ ?$$

So how shall we define $b^{(-1)}$?

ANSWER	PAGE
$b^{(-1)} = \dfrac{0}{b}$	95
$b^{(-1)} = \dfrac{1}{b}$	104

Some students and subject matters may adapt well to intrinsic programming. Certain students, for example, may find the expository frame and the multiple-choice answer more interesting than simple linear fill-in programs. Whenever the terminal behavior or subject matter calls for the assimilation of a body of information followed by a decision based on several alternatives, the Crowder frame-type seems valuable in at least one stage of the program.

Multitrack programs. In a multitrack program each frame is presented in several versions which differ in the amount of prompting used (Glaser and Schaefer, 1961). The same response is called for in all versions. For example, when three tracks are used, the top level or track A contains the version of each frame with minimum prompting. Track B versions present the same subject matter with the response more strongly cued. The greatest amount of prompting is in the C track. Until the student

Example 6.10

Track A:	The element for the blank space in the following matrix B would be called _____. $$\begin{bmatrix} 0 & 0 & 0 \\ 0 & 0 & 0 \\ 0 & 0 & \_ \end{bmatrix} = B$$
Track B:	The element for the blank space in the following matrix B would be called _____. $$\begin{bmatrix} b_{11} & 0 & 0 \\ 0 & 0 & 0 \\ 0 & 0 & b\_\_ \end{bmatrix} = B$$
Track C:	The element for the blank space in the following matrix B would be called _____. $$\begin{bmatrix} b_{11} & b_{12} & b_{13} \\ b_{21} & b_{22} & b_{23} \\ b_{31} & b_{32} & b\_\_ \end{bmatrix}$$
	Confirmation: b_{33}

can respond to one of the three tracks, response confirmation does not occur. Thus the student begins at level A. If he is sure of his response, he turns to the confirmation and continues to the next frame in the program. If he is not sure, he goes to track B. If he is still unsure, he descends to the track C frame for even stronger prompting before making his response. Example 6.10 illustrates a page from a multitrack sequence in a program on matrix algebra. Superior students should be able to proceed through the program solely on track A. The less able or less well prepared student may frequently experience difficulty on track A, but receives additional prompting in tracks B or C.

Practically, the multitrack program differs only slightly from the linear program. The important difference is in giving the student an opportunity to obtain additional prompts before he responds. Variations of this procedure are readily apparent. Multitracking might be used only for certain critical frames in an otherwise linear program, or it might be useful in review sequences to which students come with varied amounts of retention. Multitracking seems to be a useful compromise between linear and more complex branching approaches to programmed instruction, but at present it needs further examination and evaluation.

In Summary. Most of the implications and possibilities of branching in programming have not yet been explored. The use of a branching technique in no way implies that frames must be long or short or that responses must be multiple-choice or fill-in. In fact, most of the frames in the usual linear program could easily be incorporated into branching programs. Moreover, there is no reason why short and long frames, fill-in and multiple-choice answers, or branching and linear segments cannot be mixed in the same program. The choice between linear, branching, and other types of programs should hinge upon the nature of the terminal behavior requirements, the sophistication and characteristics of the student, and the conditions necessary for learning.

RESPONSE MODE

Aside from certain subject matter requirements, there are no rigid specifications for the form of behavior a program asks from the student. Psychologists hold differing opinions concerning response mode, and so far programs have used multiple-choice, true-false, constructed answer, reconstructed answer based upon scrambled material, and labeling. Responses have also been verbal and nonverbal, written and spoken, as well as overt and covert. The majority of current programs use constructed answer frames, that is, frames in which the student actually writes out his response. Constructed answers have much to recommend them, but the labor of writing out responses often may attenuate the motivational value of a program. On the other hand, the effort of writing may serve to keep some students concentrating on the responses to be made.

Multiple-choice answers are easier to score and permit automation more readily than constructed responses. However, some psychologists point out that the incorrect stimuli presented in multiple-choice answers may confuse the student or may be incidentally learned and conflict with the correct response. Multiple-choice responses are almost a requirement in intrinsic programming. They have also been used with the small step linear type of program.

Results of several experiments indicate no differences between students who construct responses and those who select multiple-choice responses. In one interesting experiment, children were taught to write numbers even though throughout the course of the program they never actually constructed a number, but merely responded to multiple-choice answers (Evans, 1961; Glaser, 1962). The children learned to write numbers fairly well, possibly because they had learned the appropriate discriminations which enabled them to monitor their first actual writing during the posttest.

Another variation in response mode is the possibility of implicit or covert responses to constructed answer frames. It would seem efficient to have the student respond to himself to a frame, without actually writing out his response. Experiments have shown that under certain circumstances this can be an effective procedure. However, implicit responding leaves no record of student responses which can be used to improve and revise the program. In certain programs, overt and covert (implicit) responding can be combined so that the student is required to respond overtly only to certain frames. Such "test" frames also help insure that the student has paid attention to the previous frames. If "working problems to oneself" is an important aspect of the subject matter, a combined frame sequence of this sort might be used to teach the student to respond implicitly.

A program need not consist exclusively of one type of response mode, of course, but can include various kinds. Although research concerning response modes is needed, it seems reasonable to employ various modes so as to increase the general interest and to adapt the program to a variety of subject matter topics. Most important, a program should call for student behavior that is as close as possible to the expert behavior for any given subject matter. For example, since draftsmen are required to produce plans and blueprints, a program for draftsmen must have the student produce this type of behavior. If an expert is required to make decisions between alternate courses of action, then the program leading to expertise must involve a kind of multiple-choice behavior.

SUMMARY

Learning programs differ in numerous respects: in the frame sequences and extra materials used, in structure and format, and in the response mode employed. Frames in a program are arranged in careful sequences to provide several learning trials for the learner and to produce specific behavioral outcomes: an introductory sequence calls out the entering repertoire upon which a program can build; a discrimination sequence limits the range of stimuli which will call out or control certain responses; a generalization sequence extends the range of controlling stimuli; a chaining sequence establishes a complex, self-sustained series of responses; and drill and review sequences enhance retention of learned material.

Various extra-frame materials or panels can be used in a program to cue or organize behavior. A variety of these materials may be used, such as pictures, illustrations, and diagrams which the student looks at, a page on which the student draws or writes, and objects which the student takes apart or assembles. Programs can also be arranged to yield a set of review notes or an abbreviated manual by calling for responses on certain frames to be entered on a special note page.

There have been two major types of programs, linear and branching. In linear programs, all students respond to every frame and move directly through the program from the first to the last frame. Branching programs allow the learner to move directly through the program as long as he responds correctly; errors branch him to supplementary material designed to correct the particular type of error made. The major use of branching has been in intrinsic programming which also uses long frames and multiple-choice responses. This type of program makes use of errors to diagnose weak spots in training. Well-motivated students, moreover, may find such a program to be more interesting than linear, short frame programs. For average students, however, the long frames may tend to decrease student participation and create sources of error. Several modifications have been proposed to increase the flexibility of a linear program. For example, a multitrack arrangement, in which different amounts of cueing are available for each frame, may be a useful compromise between linear and branching programming. In general, research to date has shown no marked advantage for simple branching as compared with linear sequences.

Current programs use numerous modes of responding; the most widely used are constructed response and multiple-choice. Multiple-choice responses are easiest to score but confront the learner with incorrect stimuli which may be a source of competition in learning the correct response. Although multiple-choice answers have been traditionally used in branching programs, they are used where desirable in small step, linear programs. Constructed responses are most frequently used in linear programs; their major drawback for the student seems to be the labor of writing. In this regard, there is some evidence that implicit or covert constructed responses under certain circumstances may be as effective as overt responding. A program need not employ just one mode of responding; any number of modes may be combined. It seems reasonable, however, to require behavior, especially towards the end of a program, that is as similar as possible to expert behavior in that subject matter.

REFERENCES

Crowder, N. A. Automatic tutoring by means of intrinsic programming. In A. A. Lumsdaine & R. Glaser (Eds.), *Teaching machines and programmed learning*. Washington: National Education Association, 1960. Pp. 286–298.

Evans, J. L. Multiple-choice discrimination programming. Paper read at American Psychological Association, New York, September, 1961.

Fundamentals of electricity. New York: Teaching Materials Corporation, 1961.

Gilbert, T. F. Mathetics: the technology of education. *J. Mathetics*, 1962, 1 (1), 7–73.

Glaser, R. Some research problems in automated instruction: instructional programming and subject matter structure. In J. E. Coulson (Ed.), *Programmed learning and computer-based instruction*. New York: Wiley, 1962. Pp. 67–85.

Glaser, R. and H. H. Schaefer. *Principles of programming printed materials*. Pittsburgh: University of Pittsburgh, 1961. Final report on Contract AF 33(616)–7175.

Holland, J. G. and B. F. Skinner. *The analysis of behavior*. New York: McGraw-Hill, 1961.

Holzman, A. G., H. H. Schaefer, and R. Glaser. *Matrices and mathematical programming: mathematical bases for management decision making*. Chicago: Encyclopaedia Britannica Press, 1962.

Markle, Susan M. *Words: a programed course in vocabulary development*. Chicago: Science Research Associates, 1962.

Mechner, F. Science education and behavioral technology. In R. Glaser (Ed.), *Teaching machines and programed learning, II: data and directions*. Washington: National Education Association, 1965.

Schaefer, H. H., A. P. Jeffries, H. F. Phillips, T. S. Harakas, and R. Glaser. *General science series*. New York: Teaching Materials Corporation, 1962.

CHAPTER SEVEN

Program Development

This chapter considers certain problems involved in the actual production of a program. It discusses the selection and use of students in program tryout, the training of programming personnel, the steps in developing the first draft of a program, problems in editing and revision, and the contents of a program manual to accompany the final published program. Each individual programmer or programming group will develop its own best production methods. The present chapter is intended only to serve as an indication of some current practices.

Selecting and Using Tryout Students

The personnel of primary importance in the programming enterprise are the students on whom the program is tried out during the various stages of its production. At the heart of program development are the data obtained on student performance. A program works if students can display the behavior called for in succeeding steps and can, at the end of the program, perform the specified terminal behavior. It is possible, by overprompting, for students to succeed at each step but to fail to attain the terminal behavior; the steps in such a program do not guide the students to the desired performance. Other inadequate programs may lead the student to the attainment of the terminal behavior but by means of overly redundant and uninteresting frames.

In essence, *the student teaches the programmer* what to do next. The student's response to each frame and his final test performance are the measures which guide the programmer in revising the program. Many programmers point out that it is the number of revisions which a program goes through that is important rather than the number of subjects on which the program is tried at any given tryout. Also, the judgment of learners regarding the frames to which they are exposed will frequently be useful. Comments may be heard such as, "I know exactly what you want to get across here, only I think I could do it much better this way . . ." It is desirable to make note of these reports.

Selecting tryout subjects. A statement of terminal behavior requires a statement of who is to perform that behavior. This is not to say that a subject matter which is conventionally taught at a particular educational or aptitude level must necessarily be confined to that level. On the contrary, it appears likely that topics taught by conventional teaching methods in certain grades or training levels can be taught earlier through programming. As has been indicated, however, it is important for the programmer to be aware of the response repertoires of the students who are to be taught. Often programmers try out their programs on available rather than upon representative subjects. While such informal tryout is useful in discovering gross errors and carelessness, it cannot tell the programmer how well he has succeeded in reaching the response repertoire of the learner for whom the program is intended.

The more a programmer knows about his tryout subjects, the more he will be able to say about the nature of the resulting program. Although it is frequently good policy to choose subjects of average intelligence for testing a program, the characteristics of the subjects should depend upon the intent of the program and whether it is planned for typical students or is adapted by some branching procedure to individual differences. It is important to assess the subject's existing response repertoire. In developing a program on meteorology, for example, it seems necessary to ascertain to what degree a student is familiar with certain general physical laws, such as the expansion and contraction of materials due to temperature changes. The selection of tryout students may be less a matter of measured aptitudes, age, and specific standing on the educational scale, and more a question of the kind of subject matter behavior which the student displays.

Programmer Training

After a period of initial instruction, it seems best to have the programmer almost immediately start writing frames. For example, he may be asked to write 25 to 50 sample frames leading to a specified bit of terminal behavior. These frames should be carefully edited to illustrate good programming techniques. The programmer should then revise his own frames or write a new sequence covering the same material. A good aid in initial instruction is the book by Markle (1964).

Editorial marks. The use of special editorial marks is especially helpful with beginning frame writers and provides an efficient means of interaction between experienced and novice programmers, since the symbols save lengthy explanations. Some illustrative editorial symbols for programming are presented below:

Я

The wrong response is likely to be emitted to this frame. This symbol may be useful in pointing out that in programming the effort is made to elicit specific behavior from the student. This effort is related to the effective use of prompts and the strength of control stimuli which influence the reader's response.

Я̷

The stimulus is too general; possibly no response will be emitted to this frame. This is similar to the preceding instance, but the frame is too general or too ambiguous to elicit a specific response.

—R→

A response previously learned to this stimulus material may intrude and produce the wrong response; existing responses are likely to interfere with the desired response here. This symbol is often used if the programmer fails to realize that a student brings many associations to the program with him.

—R—

The range of possible correct responses is too wide. Sometimes the programmer is not aware of other possible responses the student could give to the frame.

\eg/

Add an example or example frame before trying to evoke this response.

\ru/

Add a rule or a rule frame, that is, a statement of the generalization being taught. At this point it is well to explain the function of rules and examples with a statement about the construction of rule and example frames (see Chapter 5).

Ø̷

There is no need to state this frame as a question. Let the response emerge in the context rather than as an answer to a question. Beginning programmers have a tendency to ask questions after they have stated something in a frame. There is nothing wrong in proceeding this way except that if done excessively it can become aversive to the student.

Q

Insert inquiry or test for terminal behavior. This is equivalent to saying, "Fade all prompts." It is not necessarily an invitation to state the frame as a question, although sometimes this may be appropriate. If the terminal behavior is such that a lengthy response is required, it should be asked for specifically by a question rather than by a complicated completion-type frame.

!

Good use of existing response repertoire. This symbol is a reinforcing editor's mark, general in nature and quite useful. However, programmers should realize that their reinforcement comes from the fact that the subjects learn and not so much from an editor's opinion.

n⟩

Split into separate frames as marked. The symbol *n* indicates the number of frames suggested.

W

Too wordy.

RR

Too many responses. Split into several frames, or limit to one response.

These last three marks all deal with the same problem: the beginning programmer tends to write frames that are much too long. Sometimes a frame is too wordy and needs no more than editing from the point of view of good English. Other frames, however, are overloaded with stimuli and frequently require too many responses for one frame. While there seems to be nothing wrong from the psychological point of view in eliciting several responses in one frame, it often confuses the learner, especially at the beginning of a program sequence. It is no more time consuming to have several frames, each of which elicits one or a few responses, than to have one frame which elicits many responses.

|R|

This calls for a trivial response; response is already at high strength; prompting is too strong. Here the programmer elicits a response which really has nothing to do with the subject matter—responses such as "is," "is not," "and," "yet," or "no." There are times and places when responses such as these should be elicited, but only if doing so is of relevance to the terminal behavior in question.

D

Discrimination training. This symbol is seldom used by itself. It may be used with the "split-into-separate-frames-as-marked" symbol already described to indicate that the programmer should insert a series of discrimination frames. This would be suggested when it appears that the programmer has to use more frames to establish a required subject matter discrimination. See Chapter 6 for a discussion and examples of discrimination sequences.

G

Generalization. This symbol also is seldom used without additional instructions. If it is used with the "split-into-separate-frames-as-marked" symbol it indicates that the programmer should insure that the student has explored the full range or total implications of some subject matter principle. See Chapter 6 for examples of a generalization sequence.

wm

Warm-up or review frames. Sometimes a programmer assumes that more is retained from a previous section of a program than seems warranted. The warm-up symbol indicates to him that he should introduce a few frames that refer to previously learned material, usually with very little prompting. The symbol is also useful when the programmer has failed to seed review frames.

c

Consider use of chaining here. The concept of chaining has been explained in Chapter 3, and examples of the use of chaining in programming may be found in Chapter 6.

[m ... n]

Rewrite frames from m to n. This is the least specific of the editor's comments. It indicates that nothing can be done with the frames as they exist; they need to be rewritten. Usually such a mark is accompanied by another one indicating the general nature of the change that is needed.

?

Subject matter seems questionable; have an expert check.

The symbols listed above may be used by themselves or in combination. Of course, a little practice with such symbols is required in order for programmers to use them easily, but learning the symbols can be a helpful step in learning the techniques of programming.

Program Writing

Developing the first draft. It is a good idea for the beginning work on a program to sample various parts of the subject matter since the point is not so much to produce polished and useful frames as to further orient the programmer to the long-range task. Short sequences (50 to 100 frames) should be prepared leading to different samples of the terminal behavior. This will permit programmers to gain experience with different areas of the subject matter and to develop useful approaches.

At this time the programmer will want to keep in close contact with each student, perhaps even sitting with the student while the program is being worked through. Between five and ten students is a sufficient number for trying out frames at this stage. When a frame sequence has been tried out, the programmer uses the students' responses and comments as guides in revising the frames. The essential task is to analyze responses and try to understand the conditions which prevented or helped the learning process.

After the initial tryouts and subsequent rewriting, the revised frames should be tried out once more and, if necessary, rewritten until the subject matter is learned as indicated by a short test of the terminal behavior. At this point, a sequence may be considered to be in a first draft form.

First editing. After tryout and revision, consecutive program sequences can be grouped into units and edited and discussed by experts in writing style, programmed learning, and the subject matter involved. Some arbitration may be necessary. For example, it may be necessary for instructional reasons to make a statement about the subject matter which, taken out of context, is incomplete. The subject matter specialist may forget that this incomplete statement will later be elaborated upon and should not be judged out of context. In a mathematics program, for example, he may criticize the introduction of a matrix which does not have the lines or brackets on the sides to indicate that it is a matrix. Yet this may not be an unreasonable procedure at all when later frames teach the student that an array of numbers without these lines should no longer be considered a matrix. To have presented this information earlier in the program would place too sudden a burden upon the student. The subject-matter editor should understand this method of proceeding and function mainly to prevent technically incorrect *terminal* behavior from being established. The stylistic editor, too, may find that a program violates some of his principles. Repetition, although often alien to good writing procedures, may serve a specific function in a program, such as connecting one stimulus with a set of related stimuli in the course of a discrimination or generalization sequence. If revisions are drastic, it is necessary to repeat the production process to this point. If, however, the program unit has not undergone drastic change, it is prepared for further student tryout.

Program tryout. The sample of subjects who take the program at this stage is carefully selected to conform to the eventual user. From 15 to 40 or more students may be used. In contrast to the tryouts of short sequences, students should be tested on a carefully prepared, detailed diagnostic performance test after completing the program unit. For some subject matters where previous student exposure is difficult to specify, it is desirable to give a test prior to the program. Testing students before and after taking the program provides a baseline against which student performance can be assessed.

After this tryout, the frames are again analyzed and the success with which terminal behavior has been attained, as indicated on the test, is determined. The posttest can be analyzed in terms of total or part scores and the results summarized with respect to various program subunits. The analysis of student responses to program frames can be made in various ways but should at least yield a tally of the frequency with which each frame was missed and a list of common errors made. A high error rate on a particular frame often points to a need for revision, and the types of errors made indicate how the revision should proceed. Moreover, seeing the reasons for student errors can be highly instructive for both programmers and editors.

What will typically exist after the response analysis is a copy of each frame with a brief summary statement of student responses in a form such as "2/15; 9 electrical energy; 4 electricity; correct response, energy." This notation indicates that 2 out of 15 students gave the correct response "energy," 9 wrote "electrical energy," and 4 responded with "electricity." In addition, the annotated copy of the program should contain a statement by the person who had contact with the students summarizing any student comments. These materials together with the test results are reviewed in order to determine whether the program satisfactorily teaches the terminal behavior or whether further revision is required. This decision is primarily determined by the extent to which the program has enabled the students to perform well on the test of terminal behavior. At this stage the program may undergo several tryout and revision cycles.

Further Editing and Processing

Sometimes it is evident that the terminal behavior, as outlined, cannot be achieved by the method of programming originally proposed or that it can be achieved best by another method. For example, in teaching general science in a junior high school, it seemed advantageous to program the subject matter by topics. Implicit in teaching the topics was the assumption that certain common notions would be learned in all topics. In the test for the terminal behavior it was found that students gained satisfactory knowledge about each topic but were unable to generalize the concepts which the topics had in common. Thus the tryout revealed that it might have been better to break the whole program into subunits by concepts rather than by topics (Glaser, 1962). The empirical nature of programming may make it necessary to revise, sometimes extensively, past methods of teaching the subject matter.

If the terminal behavior has been achieved in the tryouts, the program may be prepared in its final form. At this stage, editing requires attention to every word, comma, period, and semicolon in each frame. Since the student's response is so carefully guided in programmed learning, the consequences of typographical errors are much more serious than in a conventional textbook.

Preparing the program format. This book has been primarily concerned with programs of the paper-and-pencil, linear, constructed-response type. Although such programs may be prepared for a machine when this provides increased learning efficiency, the most simple way to present these programs is as a programmed textbook. During tryout and early stages of production frames need not be in the final format; they may be on paper strips or film strips for use with certain machines, or they may be on separate cards.

However it is important to emphasize that the nature of the subject matter and the characteristics of the students will dictate the format in which the program appears. It is also to be pointed out that no one teaching machine or display mode will take care of all the programs that will be developed. For special skills it is sometimes useful to favor machine presentation of a program. Furthermore, a display device which is excellent for certain subject matters and with certain trainees may be much less effective when used in a different situation. Machine presentation and automated instruction have not been discussed in the scope of this book. For a discussion of the possibilities of machine and computer-based presentation, the reader is referred elsewhere (Coulson, 1962; Finn, 1963; Kopstein and Shillestad, 1961; Stolurow, 1961; Stolurow and Davis, 1965).

Final Tryout

When all the units of a program have been assembled and have been reproduced in a presentation format like that to be used in final printing, the program should be tried out once more on a group of students for whom the program is intended. This tryout is not meant to change any aspects of the program but to further validate the existing program and to determine its optimal use in an instructional setting. Students might also be assigned to experimental groups each of which use the program in a different way. This tryout may be used to indicate the best role for the instructor and the organization of the curriculum in terms of the sequence of programmed material, laboratory work, group discussion and lectures. Only after the completion of all the stages described here, including this last validation stage, can a program stand as a finished product.

THE PROGRAM MANUAL

When a program is published for operational classroom use, it should be accompanied by a manual which provides the user with adequate information about the objectives of the program, the procedures involved in its development, suggestions for its use, and descriptions of what might be expected from the program based on its previous effectiveness. Users in operational educational and training situations will have only the information supplied in the manual and will rely on it in making decisions concerning the program. The manual should be updated and revised at appropriate intervals on the basis of further use of the program. If research and development are to be conducted in connection with the program, a supplementary manual will be required for research personnel.

It is recommended that the following items be considered in the preparation of a program manual. The items listed can also serve as a checklist to help insure that a program has adhered to certain standards of quality.

Specification of Objectives:

1. The objectives should be stated as specific behaviors which can be observed in student performance. It is insufficient to say that a student should understand and be able to apply Ohm's law; situations must be specified which indicate samples of performance. The program manual should indicate how the training objectives were derived and should refer to appropriate curriculum and subject matter sources.

2. The manual should refer to specific achievement tests which measure the terminal performance taught by the program.

3. If the programming procedure has suggested new ways of presenting the subject matter, these innovations should be described. For example, if the terminal behavior is best attained by an unorthodox subject matter arrangement, the merits of this arrangement should be explained.

Program Prerequisites (Entering Behavior):

1. The knowledge and skills required by the student in order to begin the program should be clearly stated. If available, programs or other courses of instruction which prepare the student for the program under consideration should be indicated.

2. The aptitude levels of the students for whom the program is designed should be stated. These aptitude levels should be stated in terms of generally recognized aptitude tests.

3. If desirable, a test of prerequisite ability should be indicated and its use described.

Program Validity:

1. Achievement test data should be reported to indicate the extent to which the program has accomplished its instructional objectives. These

data should be reported in quantitative terms indicating the mean and standard deviation of group proficiency test scores.

2. The test(s) employed to evaluate the program should be either an appropriate standardized achievement test currently in use or a specially prepared test which adequately samples the terminal behavior.

3. The content of the achievement test should be described accurately and in detail, indicating the kind of performance it measures and the kind of performance it does not measure in relation to the above described Specification of Objectives.

Test Conditions and Student Sample:

1. The conditions under which the proficiency test was administered should be described, for example, the time interval between finishing the program and taking the test, whether more than one test was given to measure retention of the subject matter, and whether precautions were taken to avoid prior exposure to the test. If the subject matter is one in which a student could have had little prior exposure, administration of the test after the program is sufficient. If, however, the subject material is one which many students might have learned before taking the program, alternate forms of achievement tests should be given before and after program administration.

2. The sample of students on which the data have been collected should be described in detail, for example, their prior training, background, and aptitude level. Indications should be given of the extent to which the student sample departs from the kind of student for which the program is recommended.

3. The characteristics of the school or training situation in which the data have been collected should be clearly described.

Program Effectiveness:

1. Indication should be given of the efficiency of the program as an instructional tool. Frequently this can be given in terms of the time taken to attain the terminal behavior and the amount of supplementary instruction recommended for use with the program, that is, the amount of instructor time required and the amount of additional student work required.

2. The extent to which the program enlarges student knowledge should be indicated, for example, if the program teaches more than is usual or can be used with lower aptitude, age, and background levels than is usual.

3. Some indication of the effects of the program upon student motivation and work habits should be reported. The technique of programmed instruction promises to encourage more interest in the subject matter and better habits of concentration. Data on such a hypothesis should be presented as quantitatively as possible and as the result of controlled study.

4. After further experience with the program it is highly desirable to publish supplements to the manual that describe the extent to which the behavior taught in the program is retained over periods of time and is transferred to related subject matters.

Administrative Considerations:

1. The manual should describe the way in which the program is to be used in conjunction with other means of instruction such as lectures, discussion groups, or laboratory work. Indications should be given of the amount of time the student should spend on the program each day in relation to these other activities.

2. If use of the program necessitates other than the usual classroom arrangement, such recommendations should be specified.

SUMMARY

The development of a program is a lengthy process requiring much detailed analysis of data and the repeated tryout of program drafts. Most important are the students who work through the program prior to final stage. On the basis of student responses the programmer can determine the revisions necessary to make the program an effective teaching device.

An important step in any programming enterprise is the training of programmers. Programmers should begin frame writing and revising very early in their training. After the first draft of the program has been written, tried out, and revised until it is effective in teaching the subject matter, the program should be reviewed by experts in writing style and subject matter. The program should then undergo further revision on the basis of these editorial comments. During this stage the use of a detailed achievement test to assess the effectiveness of the program is essential. When the program has been finally assembled in a format like that to be used in final printing, the program should be tried out once again in order to further validate the existing program and to determine its optimal use in an instructional setting.

Each program, when completed, should be accompanied by a manual which provides information about the objectives, prerequisites, and validity of the program, suggestions for optimal use, and descriptions of what might be expected from the program based on its previous effectiveness.

REFERENCES

Coulson, J. E. (Ed.) *Programmed learning and computer-based instruction.* New York: Wiley, 1962.

Finn, J. D. Technological development: its meaning for education. In R. T. Filep (Ed.), *Perspectives in programing.* New York: Macmillan, 1963. Pp. 192–204.

Glaser, R. Some research problems in automated instruction: instructional programming and subject matter structure. In J. E. Coulson (Ed.), *Programmed learning and computer-based instruction.* New York: Wiley, 1962. Pp. 67–85.

Kopstein, F. F. and Isabel J. Shillestad. *A survey of auto-instructional devices.* Wright-Patterson Air Force Base, Ohio: Aeronautical Systems Division, 1961. Technical Report 61–414.

Markle, Susan M. *Good frames and bad.* New York: Wiley, 1964.

Stolurow, L. M. *Teaching by machine.* Washington: U. S. Government Printing Office, 1961.

Stolurow, L. M. and D. Davis. Teaching machines and computer-based systems. In R. Glaser (Ed.), *Teaching machines and programed learning, II: data and directions.* Washington: National Education Association, 1965.

CHAPTER EIGHT

Data and
Research Issues

This chapter presents some examples of the use of programmed instruction in a school system and in an industrial organization. It also discusses general research and development issues that have grown out of the use of programmed instructional materials. A greater variety of examples of results from the use of programmed instructional materials have been reported in numerous articles and books, for example, Hughes (1963), Margulies and Eigen (1962), Coulson (1962), Glaser (1965), and Ofiesh and Meierhenry (1964). Discussions are also available of pertinent issues in programmed instruction and in the application of psychological findings to educational practice, for example, Lumsdaine (1961), Glaser (1962), Hilgard (1964), DeCecco (1964). These references provide a broad coverage of work and thinking in the field.

Use in a School System

As a part of a study reported by Glaser, Reynolds, and Fullick (1963), commercially available programs were introduced as instructional materials in the curriculum of the elementary grades. Prior to the selection of programmed material, teachers, school administers, and university researchers met to discuss available programs, methods of using them, and procedures for collecting detailed data on their effectiveness. Some of the results obtained during the course of the school year are described below.

The programs employed were available from reputable program publishers. These publishers provided some evidence that the programs were constructed according to good program development practices. This evidence was frequently of an informal nature, since most program publishers at the present time do not provide manuals (of the kind suggested in Chapter 7) giving detailed program use and validity data. To a large extent this omission is a function of the newness of programs, and manuals similar to those accompanying nationally standardized tests will probably be made available in the future. Standard criteria which publishers can follow in the development of a program manual are being developed by a national committee (Joint Committee on Programed Instruction and Teaching Machines, 1963; Lumsdaine, 1965). The common type of program on the school market is the linear program in which all students go through the same materials and no provision is made for branching sequences. In the study to be reported, all programs used were linear in format.

The subject matters taught were selected on the basis of the availability of programs, subject matter requirements for the particular grade levels involved and student-teacher-community acceptance as determined by the school administrators. The programs were considered as representative of the subject matter normally taught at the grade levels in which they were introduced.

The teachers involved were chosen on the basis of their interest in trying out programmed instructional materials and participated in the development of the procedures to be used; one teacher at each grade level prepared a manual for all the teachers involved. This manual consisted of a day-by-day plan of specific classroom activities. The exact manner in which a program was to be used was described and the use of related materials for nonprogrammed instruction was specified.

In assessing the outcomes of instruction, three types of measures were employed at various times, namely, program tests, teacher-made tests, and nationally standardized tests. Program tests are achievement tests which the program publisher considers an adequate sample of student performance to measure the objectives taught by the program. Teacher-made tests are developed in cooperation with the classroom teacher and consist of items representative of the expressed educational objectives of classroom instruction. Nationally standardized tests are those commercially available achievement tests used by schools to assess their instruction and compare themselves with national norms. All three of these types were employed in the various studies reported, although they may not be described in the illustrative data presented below. Where the program test was not considered an adequate test of overall classroom objectives or of the program itself, it was supplemented by a teacher test or by a nationally standardized test. When a nationally standardized test was used, agreement was obtained from the teacher and school administrators that this test was an adequate measure of their own course objectives.

Measuring student mastery. In this connection, some general remarks can be made about the measurement of instructional outcomes. If a definitive test is established to indicate mastery of course objectives, then the objectives of instruction are to teach so that students attain such mastery. This means that in successful instruction many students will obtain perfect scores and the distribution of scores obtained for a class will be skewed with a ceiling imposed by perfect test performance. If two different instructional treatments are given to two different groups and both groups show many students with near perfect test scores, the problem is to distinguish which treatment represents the more effective instruction. Factors other than student achievement must be considered, such as time taken to attain mastery, etc. If achievement is the measure of concern, then the percentage of students obtaining a perfect score, the average level of mastery, or the gain in mastery from pre- to posttesting can be used. A question might always remain, however, with respect to how much more knowledge would have been exhibited by students if the test did not have a mastery ceiling. For example, if the objective of a course of instruction is to teach students addition and subtraction with single-digit numbers, a mastery test would measure just that skill—addition and subtraction with single-digit numbers; however, it is justifiable to ask to what extent students can extrapolate and transfer their knowledge to two- and three-place numbers. The tests employed in the school studies reported here were, for the most part, tests with mastery ceilings and were used to assess the attainment of specific mastery objectives. Sometimes tests of more general objectives were employed which did not display ceiling effects. There were usually nationally standardized tests which are constructed so as to give a wide distribution of scores.

First grade arithmetic. In the beginning weeks of first grade, an exploratory study was conducted to determine how well very young students could work independently on programmed instructional materials. The program used taught the students to write and to recognize the numerals from 1 to 10, to associate numerals with number of objects, and to discriminate between numerals. Students worked for approximately 20 minutes each day. A pretest measuring the program objectives was given prior to beginning the program, and the same test was given to each student as he completed the program. Each student progressed through the program at his own pace. The distribution of completion times, shown in Fig. 1, ranged from 8 to 25 days, indicating that the slowest

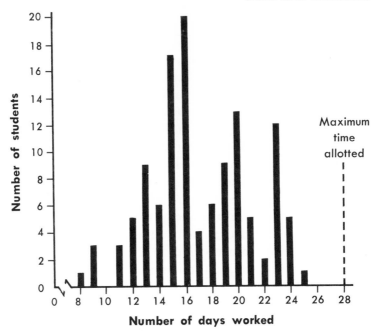

FIGURE 1. Number of days to complete introduction to numbers program
(N = 121; total possible correct = 40).

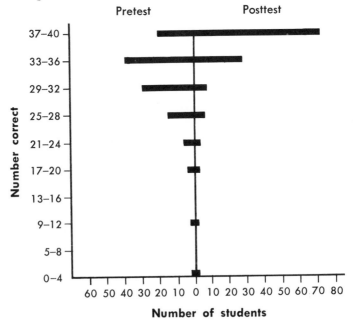

FIGURE 2. Pre- and posttest scores on introduction to numbers program
(N = 121).

student needed a little more than three times as much time to complete the program as the fastest. Pre- and posttest scores are shown in Fig. 2; this figure shows two frequency distributions of test scores. The numbers on the vertical axis refer to the score a student made on the test. The score is the number of items correct. On the horizontal axis, two sets of numbers are plotted, one for the pretest and one for the posttest. Zero for both tests begins on the center line. Taking the pretest, for example, zero begins at the line, and the numbers increase as they go to the left. The distribution of pretest scores, then, is shown to the left of the center line. This shows that, on the pretest, perfect or almost perfect scores, between 37 and 40, were obtained by 20 of the 121 students in the study. The distribution to the right of the center line shows the posttest scores and indicates that after the program 75 students received scores between 37 and 40. This figure indicates that these students were successful in learning the material taught by the program. However, many of them knew much of the material to begin with. Figure 3 shows a scatter diagram of time to complete the program and final score and indicates that there

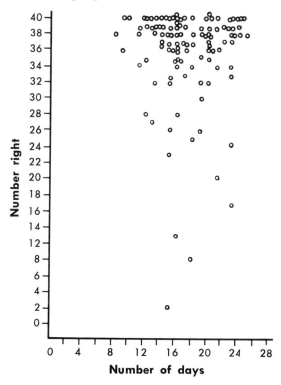

FIGURE 3. Scatter plot of final test scores and number of days to complete introduction to numbers program.

was little correlation between these two factors, that is, the students who completed the program in the shortest period of time were not necessarily those who achieved the highest posttest score.

Later in the semester students in this same group used a program in addition and subtraction. The program was used in an experiment designed to study procedures for coordinating teacher instruction and programmed self-study activity. The program taught single-digit addition and subtraction facts, and classes were scheduled for two 20-minute periods of arithmetic instruction per day, one period in the morning and one in the afternoon. One group of students (the alternation group) received alternating teacher and programmed instruction. The students worked on the program by themselves through an assigned number of frames during the morning, and in the afternoon the teacher reviewed the material covered in the program. A second group (the total program group) received only the program during both daily sessions for the first half of the study, working on the program in both morning and afternoon until it was completed; following this the teacher reviewed all of the addition and subtraction facts during both daily sessions for the remainder of the study.

Test results show that the "alternation group," which was initially higher on the pretest, scored significantly higher on the posttest, but that the two groups were equal in the amount of learning gained during the

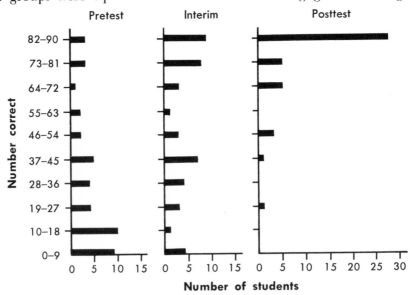

FIGURE 4. Pre-, and post-, and interim test distributions for addition and subtraction, total program group (N = 43).

course of the program. Data for the "total program group" are shown in Fig. 4. The distribution marked *interim* shows scores on a test, identical to the pre- and posttests, given to this group immediately after they completed the program and prior to teacher instruction. These scores point out that this program did not teach as effectively as could be expected, and that while some students attained mastery with it, the role of the teacher, as indicated by the posttest distribution (after both program and teacher instruction), insured proficiency in the subject matter for many more students.

Fourth grade arithmetic. At the fourth-grade level, students were given a program which taught multiplication and division facts through operations with two-place numbers. Over a six-week period, students worked through the program at their own paces during 45-minute sessions on Monday, Tuesday, Thursday, and Friday. The programmed material was divided into ten sections, and as the student completed a section he was given a written test. If he failed to achieve a score of 70% on any section he was required to go through the program again and pass a retest at the 70% level. Wednesdays were set aside for teacher instruction periods, and at this time the teacher presented review and practice materials relevant to the parts of the program which most students had completed.

Figure 5 shows pre- and posttest results when this required mastery level procedure was used. Pretest data indicate that some students knew much

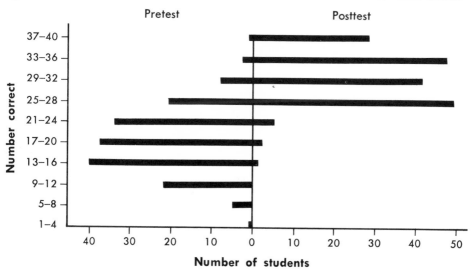

FIGURE 5. Pre- and posttest scores on multiplication and division test (N = 173).

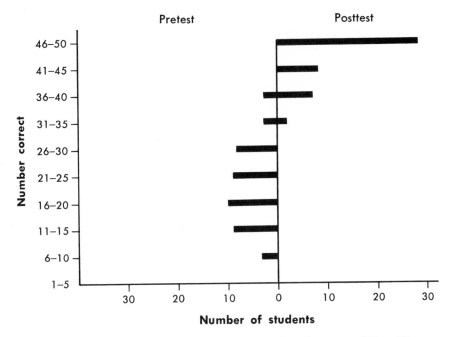

FIGURE 6. Pre- and posttest scores on fractions test (N = 45).

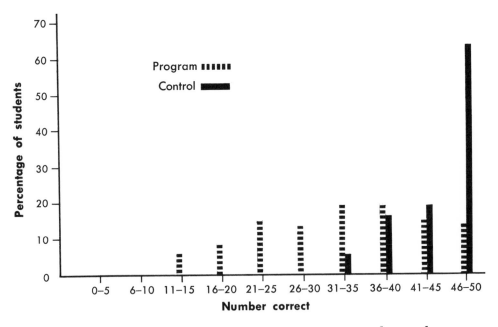

FIGURE 7. Posttest scores for fractions program group and control groups following regular curriculum.

of the program while others may not have mastered the prerequisite behavior necessary to profit from the program. However, posttest data indicate that this was a fairly effective procedure for using the program and that 96% of the students reached a level of at least 65% mastery.

After completing the multiplication and division program, the participating classes were divided into two groups. One followed the arithmetic curriculum that was currently being used by the school system for the remainder of the school year. The second group was given programmed instruction in fractions. This constituted an acceleration of the arithmetic curriculum, since fractions was normally not a part of the fourth-grade subject matter in the school participating in the study. The two groups were matched on Otis IQ and previous arithmetic achievement: Fig. 6 shows pre- and posttest distributions for the fractions group; Fig. 7 shows posttest score distributions on the fractions test for the group taking the fractions program compared with the group that followed the regular curriculum. Both of these figures would indicate that the fractions program was an effective teaching device. At the end of the school year, both of these groups were given tests in multiplication and division, and in fractions. Test data indicate no difference between the two groups in multiplication and division performance, indicating that the fractions group, which spent less time on multiplication and division, reached an achievement level equal to that of the other group. On the fractions test, the fractions group did much better than the other group, as could be expected. In general, it seems that the eight weeks of arithmetic periods spent by the fractions group in learning additional advanced material, necessarily taking away learning time from the regular arithmetic curriculum did not detract from their learning of the usual fourth-grade arithmetic topics. This strongly suggests that extension of the curriculum with programmed material produced a significant amount of additional arithmetic learning without being detrimental to the learning of material in the standard curriculum.

Fourth grade spelling. Six classes in the fourth grade received programmed instruction in spelling, using a programmed text which taught 354 new words. All classes worked on assigned frames during scheduled 20-minute class periods on Monday, Tuesday, and Wednesday of each week. On Thursday the teacher directed review and enrichment periods, and on Friday students received a written test of words covered during the week. Pre- and post-instructional spelling competence was assessed in this study by means of both a test designed specifically for the program and the spelling section of the Iowa Test of Basic Skills, a more general, standardized test. Figure 8 shows pre- and posttest distribu-

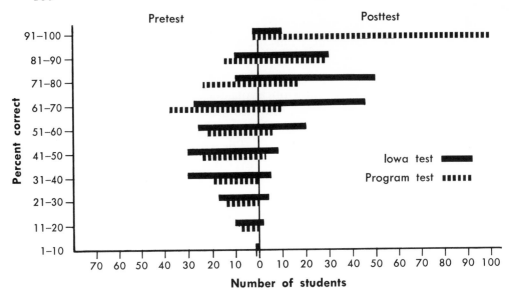

FIGURE 8. Pre- and posttest distributions on spelling section of Iowa Test of Basic Skills and program test (N = 169).

tions on these two tests. These data indicate that 65% of the students achieved a score of 90% or higher on the specific program test and in addition were quite successful on the nationally standardized test. The performance of a control group receiving traditional spelling instruction was also measured with these two examinations; this comparison showed no differences in the performances of the two groups on the Iowa Test. However, the control group was less successful than the program group on the program test. This test contained many words which the control group did not encounter in the course of their regular fourth-grade instruction. While this explains the lower control group performance on the program test, it also indicates that the program group, by being required to do so, was able to learn additional spelling words.

An Example from Industry

Holt (1963) reports a study in which basic electricity was taught to trainees at the Bell Telephone Laboratories. One group (C) was taught by the standard lecture-discussion method; the other (X) was taught the same material through a program designed specifically for this course. The primary objective of the study was to compare the effects of method C and method X on the proficiency of telephone technicians being trained in basic electricity. The comparison was made on the basis of a

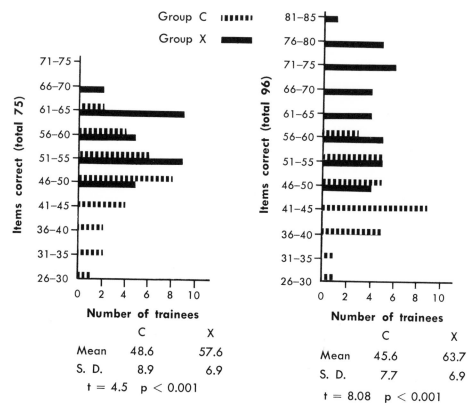

FIGURE 9. Distribution of scores on facts examination immediately after training.

FIGURE 10. Distribution of scores on concepts examination immediately after training.

criterion test taken immediately after training and again six months after completion of training. This test consisted of two parts: (1) a facts examination consisting of 75 multiple choice and completion items, and (2) a concepts examination designed to measure the trainees' ability to manipulate electrical concepts in "situational" type test items.

Before beginning the study it was determined that both groups were equivalent on measures of intelligence, knowledge of basic electricity, pretraining in mathematics and electricity, and years of company service. The results of the administration of the facts examination immediately after training are shown in Fig. 9. The results of the administration of the concepts examination are shown in Fig. 10. The difference between the means of the two sets of data is statistically significant in favor of the self-instruction group. Figures 11 and 12 show the scores of the two groups

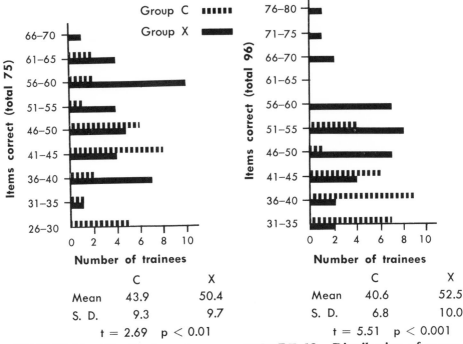

FIGURE 11. Distribution of scores on facts examination six months after completion of training.

FIGURE 12. Distribution of scores on concepts examination six months after completion of training.

on these two tests six months after completion of training. These longer range data show that the statistically significant differences between the means of the C and X groups which were found immediately after training were maintained during the retention interval although the mean scores of both groups dropped over the course of time.

For the most part, the illustrations of the use of programs in schools and industrial training have considered programs that are successful teaching instruments. It is true that there are many programs available whose effectiveness has not been so carefully documented and may not yield results comparable to those reported here. However, it would serve little purpose to report the methods by which a poor program can be implemented for instruction. Specifically, the above illustrations attempt to make four basic points: (1) The effects of programmed instruction can be usefully reported by comparing pre- and posttest score distributions. The juxtaposition of such pre and post data can give a graphic account of the degree of instructional success or failure. (2) In such evaluation, special attention must be paid to pretest performance (entering behavior).

It may be found that many students already know the material or do not have the prerequisites to begin learning it. (3) Also of special importance is the nature of the test by which a program is evaluated. Different outcomes can be obtained depending upon whether one uses the test published by the program publisher, a test made by the teacher, or a nationally standardized test in the general subject matter area. (4) In addition to subject matter competence, other behavioral characteristics of the program, such as its effect over a retention period, should be considered in its evaluation.

RESEARCH AND DEVELOPMENT ISSUES

With respect to programmed instruction, the thesis of this book can be summarized as follows: (1) The underlying concepts of programmed instruction are of primary importance in contrast to their present crude implementation. (2) Programmed instruction represents a small step in the technological application of science to educational practice. (3) As a technological application, it is under pressure to make a practical difference in instructional methodology. (4) The attempt to make a practical difference in human learning will feed information back to the behavioral scientist and open up many research questions.

Parametric Baseline Data

The first part of this chapter has presented some evaluative studies of programmed instruction. It is necessary to point out in evaluating an instructional procedure, however, that comparisons with the existing state of affairs may not be especially informative or helpful in further development. What is most useful are data on some absolute scale of just how much students actually accomplish in a subject matter, the rate at which they learn it, how long they usually remember it, etc. Just as an engineer can give some available figure on the amount of production and yield when certain techniques are used, it is necessary for educators to obtain baseline information on student performance. This should be done, not in normative terms where performance is measured in relation to the group average, but rather in behavioral terms such as size of vocabulary, the kind of arithmetic problems that can be solved, etc. Such baseline data provide a mark for evaluation and a mark to exceed.

The idea being expressed here has been referred to as the carrying out of parametric studies (Carroll, 1960) because such studies would seek to define the parameters of the learning process and would allow us to state, for example, that a given person with a specified degree of aptitude and background would take so long to reach a specified degree of subject matter competence. The question of the evaluation of programmed instructional procedures forces such studies.

Terminal Behavior Analysis

As indicated in Chapter 4, while much time has been spent on the analysis of curricula and educational goals, less time has been spent in pinpointing the kinds of performances that students must display to indicate achievement of those goals. One reason for this is that not enough is known about the analysis of complex behavior such as creativity and problem solving to allow the educator to be as specific as could be desired. A second reason, however, is that the generality of instructional procedures has not forced the delineation of performance standards which are to be attained. In contrast, the development of a programmed instructional sequence requires the programmer to analyze the characteristics of terminal performance. It is perhaps this one thing, the behavioral specificity of objectives, that may account for the success of curriculum redesign based on programmed instructional concepts. Apparently less influential in the present state of knowledge are particular variations in the nature of response characteristics, for example, free response or multiple-choice, as the learner goes through a sequence. Along the lines indicated in Chapter 4, much attention needs to be paid to the development of procedures for the analysis of terminal behavior.

The notion of behavioral specificity for educational objectives need not necessarily imply that an instructional procedure trains all students to react in the same way under similar circumstances. Work is going on, and should be continued, with programs that are designed to take students to the brink of creativity and to encourage problem solving in new situations (Crutchfield and Covington, 1963). It is conceivable that programs which take account of past backgrounds can be designed to produce student heterogeneity rather than uniformity of performance.

Subject Matter Task Properties and the Learning Process

Chapter 4 also points out that the requirement to carefully specify instruction in terms of human performance has forced the psychologist to consider the development of a taxonomy for behavioral description (Melton, 1959; Melton, 1964). A related problem that arises when one starts to build an instructional sequence is an analysis of the subject matter domain to be covered. In acquiring subject matter competence, both the structure of the subject matter, that is, its logical and epistomological arrangement, and the learning structure are involved. Learning structure dictates the kind of sequencing and ordering of subject matter stimuli and responses that have been discovered to produce certain kinds of behavior, such as retention, concept manipulation, etc. The task for research and development is (a) to study the relationship between the characteristics of subject matter tasks and the properties of the learning process which are required in order to effectively teach the performance of these tasks, and (b) to incorporate these appropriate learning structures with the epistomological structure of the subject matter domain in order to produce a more ideal acquisition of knowledge.

Performance Limits of Learning

A further aspect of instructional objectives is the question of expanding the capabilities of human performance. Presumably, as educational techniques become more effective, more of the abilities of human beings will be tapped, and new levels of performance will be reached. The concept of guiding human behavior (Chapter 3), with its emphasis on shaping and extending behavior beginning with available repertoires and proceeding to more complex objectives, can test performance limits. This can be done, for example, by teaching presently taught subject matters at earlier grade levels and by teaching aspects of behavior which have been formerly classed as aptitudes.

Assessment of Entering Behavior and Aptitude

The behavior brought to the instructional situation by the student consists of the initial repertoire, aptitudes, and prior educational attainment with which the instructional process begins. It has been pointed out in Chapter 4 that the explicitness of program development requires the assessment of these initial behaviors so that they can be used as the basis on which to guide learning. With this necessity for specifying entering behavior, the diagnostic assessment of subject matter prerequisites must become more and more precise. This raises the problem of developing an improved methodology for diagnostic achievement testing and of using this preinstructional information for guidance and motivation in the learning process. It may happen that for the purposes of a particular instructional course, the requisite entering behaviors may be diagnosed as not present in the student's entering repertoire. If such is the case, the student may be directed to acquire certain proficiencies before proceeding. The individual's entering behavior may also recommend one instructional sequence rather than another. The practical question for instructional guidance is whether the present competencies of the student can be used to get him where he would like to go and whether he can get there at this point in his development. The probable outcome of the interaction between entering behavior and the educational process or processes to be employed can be used for making a prediction about the probabilities for educational accomplishment. In this sense, aptitudes may be defined as the initial behaviors with which the instructional process must start. There is much to be done along these lines, since there has not been research which provides ready answers to the difficult problem of establishing relationships between aptitudes, including the general aptitude of measured intelligence, and the ways in which an individual learns.

The fact that a programmed instructional sequence can be used as an experimental "apparatus" makes it useful as a research tool in studies of individual differences. For example, experimental tasks can be taught to bright children and the behavior with which they enter and leave the program can be carefully identified. A group of retarded children with similar entering competence levels might then be brought to the same level of achievement as the bright students; this could be done by changing the properties of the program required to accomplish appropriate instructional steps. In this way it may be possible to operationally identify the differences between the properties of the instructional sequence required for these different groups of students.

As has been indicated elsewhere in this book, experimental work in programming has attacked the problem of constructing programs to produce certain behaviors which might be classed as aptitudes, that is, the kind of behavior measured on aptitude tests. For example, instructional programs have investigated the teaching of musical pitch discrimination (Skinner, 1961), and spatial visualization, as in translating between two- and three-dimensional figures (Brinkman, 1963). The concept of programmed instruction, with its emphasis on the development of behaviors in the individual, may permit research inroads into the analysis of behaviors which are usually not part of the school curriculum and may lead to a more rigorous definition of "aptitude."

Instructional Sequencing

This book has indicated that the development of an instructional sequence is accomplished on the basis of some knowledge of findings from the science of learning plus a good deal of practical experience, ingenuity, and empirical testing. The basic structure of present day programmed instructional sequences is a progression of behavioral steps which takes the student through to the attainment of a complex subject matter repertoire. The nature of these instructional progressions in terms of both the stimulus materials displayed to the student and the way in which he interacts with and responds to them are a fundamental issue of learning research and instructional technology. Some of the aspects of instructional sequencing which have arisen in work on programmed instruction are discussed below.

Size of Step

An instructional progression consists of steps which bring the student closer and closer to subject matter competence. The apparent "spoon feeding" which steps seem to represent is often more apparent to the subject matter expert reviewing the program than to the student taking the program. Nevertheless, the nature of a step requires study because the meaning of "step" and "step size" is, for the most part, ambiguous (Lumsdaine, 1960). For example, a step may be defined in terms of the probability of a correct response, small steps resulting in a high probability of correct responding as one proceeds through a program progression. Step size may also refer to the amount of material which the student must read before making a response or to the number of responses made before knowledge of performance is given to the student. There should be some optimal size "bite" which will be most efficient; such bites are probably different for different subject matters and for different entering behaviors. A teaching machine might be built which hunts in an adaptive way to adjust step size to an individual. At the present time, however, most program constructers act as if uniform steps are the most efficient for both the program builder and the student. The advantage to be gained by more individual adjustment is a matter for investigation.

Chapter 5 points out that there is no special rationale for the short two- or three-sentence frames currently in vogue. The same principles of learning might be applied to much grosser units if these were the most effective way to attain the desired terminal behavior. Size of step cannot be considered in isolation from other properties of the step such as those considered below.

Providing Richness of Experience

It is an advantage for the student to have experience brought to him. As the amount of knowledge in a subject matter grows, the codifying and transmitting of well-sampled experiences become very important for the instructional enterprise. A rich program should permit the student to work on a subject matter in a variety of contexts. Keen discriminations and the ability to differentiate and generalize between concepts can be guided in this way. For example, a thorough mastery of the concept "noun" occurs when the student works with material that requires the use of various kinds of nouns in contexts in which they must be discriminated from other parts of speech. Chapter 6 suggests how graded sequences should be able to teach discrimination and generalization between classes of concepts. Appropriate use of specific situations can provide the student with a repertoire which is applicable to a wide variety of situations. Research and development on programmed learning should accept as a major problem for investigation the study of the properties of student response to a graded sequence of instances which lead to effective use of the generalized and more abstract concept or rule involved.

The Form of Student Response

There has been much controversy on the manner in which a student should respond to a program (Chapter 6). For example, experimental studies have sought to contrast the effectiveness of constructed versus multiple-choice responses; no conclusive differences have been found. The assumptions of programming procedures do not make any one kind of responding any more correct than another—response mode is a function of the desired terminal behavior. For program construction, however, the form and encoding of responses can be an important matter, since some forms of response are easier to code, evaluate, and automate than others. The important research and development problem involved is the determination of the degree of generalization between different forms of response to subject matter stimuli. In the study by Evans (1961), for example, children could construct (write) numbers after making *only* multiple-choice discrimination responses in which they circled the correct matching response or pushed a button to select the correct choice. This study indicated that learning discriminations in one response mode apparently permitted the student to monitor his own behavior when different responses were required by the same stimuli.

Learning Rate

A great deal has been written about the fact that with present day programmed instructional techniques the learner can proceed at his own rate. This aspect has been proclaimed as one of the substantial advantages of programmed self-instruction. It is an advantage, especially if considered in the light of a deemphasis of lock step curricula and as a contribution to the notion that for different individuals equal educational attainments can take unequal amounts of time.

From another point of view, programmed instruction can provide an opportunity for *not* permitting students to go at their own rate and, in fact, pacing them so that they learn at a fast rate and learn to work at a fast rate wherever this is desirable. For example, under the pressure of an external or self-imposed deadline, an individual works rapidly and often produces a product that is equal or superior to what he would have done had he worked more leisurely. Little basic research work has been done on pacing during learning, and consideration of it can have both technological and scientific interest.

Response Feedback and Reinforcement

Although response feedback and reinforcement have been central concepts in this book, knowledge of the effects of these variables is quite incomplete, and investigation of the utilization of reinforcing feedback and the factors that influence it is a significant area of ongoing research. The influence of variables such as the amount, schedule, and delay of reinforcement, which have significant effects in the learning laboratory, need to be appropriately placed in the context of subject matter instruction. Furthermore, reinforcement is not an average matter, and the same instructional environment may have different reinforcement properties for different students. An interesting problem is the development of methodology whereby a learner can adjust an instructional sequence so that it is optimally reinforcing for him. Related to this latter problem is investigation of the nature of reinforcement that is produced as a result of prior performance, that is, response-produced reinforcement as described in Chapter 2. The activities the student carries out in the course of learning can become ends in themselves and are "intrinsically" reinforcing, perhaps in the same sense that a student is reinforced when he is led to discover something and make what he considers an ingenious response to a situation. A major concept in programmed instruction is the presentation of a stimulus situation which has a high probability of eliciting desired performance; this provides the foundation for an intrinsically reinforcing state of affairs. In this sense the steps in a programmed sequence can be "peaked" to an optimum of difficulty, that is, made neither too easy nor too difficult. Such programming would provide a setting for a self-reinforcing learning step. When an instructional sequence is constructed for use with a large number of subjects, each step is not quite peaked for the individual learner and hence he may require confirming feedback. Programmed sequences can probably be made more intrinsically reinforcing if they are designed so that the individual can select a learning step which most likely assures him of making an appropriate response. The term "adaptive programming" has connoted this kind of adjustment to individual differences, and experimental work with computer-based instructional systems suggests that computer capability is a possibility for handling the adjustment to individual instructional requirements. The important problem for research and development involved here is investigation of the dimensions along which an instructional situation can be individualized, such as rate of learning, mode of responding, content of examples, etc.

A problem related to the above is the study of the nature of reinforcing events in various instructional situations. For example, recent work with programmed instruction in the primary grades suggests that for bright children the aspect of a program which is most reinforcing is being permitted to go on to the next step. For these children, observing that their response is correct may not constitute a highly reinforcing event, since they have a history of being correct most of the time. With retarded children, on the other hand, the important reinforcing event in the same program is the confirming feedback that tells them they are getting certain responses correct. For the retarded children, response confirmation is highly reinforcing, since they have frequently had a history of failure in the subject being taught.

Among experimental psychologists, much work has been done on the effect of the pattern and schedule of reinforcing contingencies. This work takes account of the fact that reinforcing events can occur in different frequencies and in different patterns in the course of learning. For example, studies have indicated that the behavior of individuals matches the proportion of reinforcement to nonreinforcement of a learning task so that the probability of the response will approach the probability of reinforcement. To illustrate, if 90% of English nouns encountered by a student form their plurals in 's' and 10% with 'n,' the student would be expected to form the plural of newly encountered nouns with 's' about 90% of the time (Estes, 1960). Such relationships require intensive investigation in the context of the science of learning and also for appropriate practical implementation. In general, as pointed out in Chapter 2, the concept of reinforcement and how reinforcers operate are central in learning and instruction, and the variables involved require extensive analysis.

Measuring Learning Outcomes

The concept of programmed instruction demands that programs be accompanied by carefully prepared tests of instructional attainment. These tests serve two purposes: first, they present quite specifically a sample of the terminal behavior that the program was designed to teach. Secondly, they show, on the basis of previous program tryout, what the expected achievement can be for a particular population of students. The final frames in a program consist of samples of subject matter situations which the student must handle at the end of the instructional sequence; a relevant achievement test is then considered as representing another sample from the universe of subject matter content. In the context of programmed instruction, therefore, the development of appropriate achievement tests takes on special significance, and the requirements of programmed instruction force a reexamination of the general concepts of achievement testing.

Underlying the concept of achievement assessment is the assumption that there is a continuum of subject matter competence ranging from low proficiency to high proficiency. A student's performance occurs at some point along this continuum as measured by the behavior he displays during testing. The standard with which an individual's performance can be compared consists of the behaviors which define the points along the underlying achievement continuum. Performance levels can be established at appropriate points in the course of instruction where it is necessary to obtain information about the adequacy of student achievement. The behaviors which define each level of proficiency can be identified and established as a criterion to define the subject matter skills that a student is capable of performing when he achieves a particular level. In this sense, performance measures can be "criterion referenced" in terms of specific accomplishment which occurs along a continuum of proficiency. In contrast to criterion-referenced measures, where the performance of an individual is compared with specific subject matter competences, achievement assessment in schools is most frequently expressed in terms of "norms" where the student's performance is compared with the performance of other individuals. In much of current practice, an individual's relative standing is the primary information required, and reference is not made to subject matter content and associated performance criteria. "Grading on a curve" is a notorious example of the extreme of this practice. While normative information is certainly of practical use, measures referenced in terms of norms provide little information about the degree of student achievement in terms of what behavior he can actually perform. Norm-referenced measures supply information that one student is more or less proficient than another but do not provide information about how proficient either student is with respect to the specified terminal behavior of instruction. With increasing application of the concepts of programmed instruction, criterion-referenced scores should become more frequently employed, and the development of measurement procedures for these kinds of scores should be undertaken in a research and development effort.

Machines, the Marketplace, and the Profession

The history of the machine aspects of programmed instruction is an interesting story. The original programs designed by Skinner employed simple mechanical devices to display program frames and to receive student responses. Pressey's early work also used a simple mechanical unit. In one of the first national conferences on teaching machines, it was indicated (Homme and Glaser, 1959) that what was being accomplished by most existing devices could probably be accomplished by a programmed textbook format. This emphasis was warranted at that time to make the point that the programming of subject material was the essential ingredient and that the machine aspects, however desirable, were supplementary and useful only as they accomplished instructional functions to produce appropriate learning. Skinner made this emphasis explicit in his early papers while at the same time employing illustrative devices. However, this did not prevent a rash of commercial hardware from appearing on the market for which few programmed materials were available. A recent business survey in *Dun's Review* entitled "Programmed Learning: Return to Reality" (Buckley, 1964) discusses the disappointment of industry with teaching machines and programmed textbooks as a potential market, but also describes how programmed materials (essentially programmed textbooks) have been beneficial in industrial training. A further ominous portent is the fact that papers at professional meetings with programmed instruction in their titles are less numerous than they were a few years ago.

It is useful in concluding this book to consider the three aspects indicated above—machines, general adoption, and professional activity—in some perspective.

1. *Machines and automation.* It has been repeatedly emphasized throughout this book that instructional methodology must consider both subject matter properties and learning characteristics. The stimuli for some subject matter can be displayed by print on paper, and the response

to them can be made by a pen or pencil. The stimuli for other subject matter may require the display of sound and ideally the detection of correct vocal responses. The subject matter of reading, for example, might profit from a programmed talking typewriter (Moore, 1964). The learning of mathematical functions (Licklider, 1962), the prosodic features of speech (Lane and Buiten, 1964), the teaching of stenotypy (Uttal, 1962), and the teaching of pitch discrimination (Skinner, 1961), might require special display and response equipment for programmed instruction. In general, with the advances of modern technology in man-machine interaction and in the use of on-line computer functions (Coulson, 1962), only the most unimaginative can fail to see the significance of the "machine" in instruction. However, this hardware will not be on-the-shelf, available projection devices or simple all-purpose audio-visual aids, but will be developed especially with consideration for the properties of the subject matter being taught.

2. *General adoption.* It seems fair to say that, with only few exceptions, no publisher of programmed textbook materials has offered school systems an integrated, well-organized, graded curriculum series. What has been available, for the most part, are short sequences to be used at best as supplementary texts. Nowhere has there been a set of programmed instructional materials in which there is the continuity and coverage provided as there is, for example, in a basal reading series for the elementary schools. These reading series are replete with texts, workbooks, tests, teacher's manuals, and even associated hardware. As indicated in this book, production of a programmed instructional series with its emphasis on empirical development and the submission of evidence of effectiveness would admittedly be more expensive than the usual school textbook series, but probably very significantly less than the effort and expense devoted to the development of modern curricula going on throughout the country in many subject matter fields. After prototypes, production costs are usually drastically reduced. Programmed instructional materials, then, probably have not had as widespread adoption as publishers thought would occur because the schools demand more useful packages than have been available.

3. *Professional activity.* The implicit thesis of this book has been that probably the best thing that could happen to programmed instruction is that it become integrated into research and development in human learning and into educational psychology. This appears to be what is happening, except for a number of staunch enthusiasts who too early in the development of programmed instruction have attempted to separate

technology from scientific research and would like technological prac-
titioners to stand on their own. This of course is hardly possible or
desirable at the present time. What appears to be happening, as indicated
by the literature in the field, is that work in programmed instruction has
raised many questions about the relationship between psychological
knowledge and educational practice, and researchers have investigated
these problems with primary regard for their particular disciplinary
interests, assimilating the concepts of programmed instruction with no
special necessity for setting up a special field labeled "programmed instruction." For the present, programs will continue to be built for educational and research purposes along the lines indicated in this book,
but with the increasing interest in the scientific bases of instruction that
programmed instruction has helped engender, the shape of things will certainly change. As this happens, the science of learning, educational
psychology, and educational practice will develop a mutual relevance.

REFERENCES

Brinkman, E. H. Educability in visualization of objects in space: a programmed instruction approach. Unpublished doctoral dissertation,
Univer. of Michigan, 1963.

Buckley, N. Programmed learning: return to reality. *Dun's Review,*
1964.

Carroll, J. B. Wanted: a research basis for educational policy on foreign
language teaching. *Harvard educ. Rev.,* 1960, **30** (2), 128–140.

Coulson, J. E. (Ed.) *Programmed learning and computer-based instruction.* New York: Wiley, 1962.

Crutchfield, R. S. and M. V. Covington. Facilitation of creative thinking
and problem solving in school children. Paper read at American Assn.
for the Advancement of Science, Cleveland, December 29, 1963.

DeCecco, J. P. (Ed.) *Educational technology.* New York: Holt, Rinehart & Winston, 1964.

Estes, W. K. Learning. *Encyclopedia of educational research* (3rd ed.)
New York: Macmillan, 1960. Pp. 752–767.

Evans, J. L. Multiple-choice discrimination programming. Paper read
at Amer. Psychol. Assn., New York, September, 1961.

Glaser, R. (Ed.) *Training research and education.* Pittsburgh: Univ. of
Pittsburgh Press, 1962.

Glaser, R. (Ed.) *Teaching machines and programed learning, II: data
and directions.* Washington: Natl. Education Assn., 1965.

Glaser, R., J. H. Reynolds, and Margaret G. Fullick. *Programmed instruction in the intact classroom.* Pittsburgh: University of Pittsburgh, 1963.

Hilgard, E. R. (Ed.) *Theories of learning and instruction: Sixty-third Yearbook of the National Society for the Study of Education.* Chicago: Univ. of Chicago Press, 1964.

Holt, H. O. An exploratory study of the use of a self-instruction program in basic electricity. In J. L. Hughes (Ed.), *Programed learning: a critical evaluation.* Chicago: Educational Methods, 1963. Pp. 15–39.

Homme, L. E. and R. Glaser. Relationships between the programmed textbook and teaching machines. In E. Galanter (Ed.), *Automatic teaching: the state of the art.* New York: Wiley, 1959.

Hughes, J. E. (Ed.) *Programed learning: a critical evaluation.* Chicago: Educational Methods, 1963.

Joint Committee on Programed Instruction and Teaching Machines. Criteria for assessing programed instructional materials. *Audiovisual Instruction,* 1963, (**8**), 84–89.

Lane, H. L. and R. L. Buiten. Preliminary manual for the speech auto-instructional device. Unpublished report, Ann Arbor: Univ. of Michigan, 05613-2-P, 1964.

Licklider, J. C. R. Preliminary experiments in computer-aided teaching. In J. E. Coulson (Ed.), *Programmed learning and computer-based instruction.* New York: Wiley, 1962. Pp. 217–239.

Lumsdaine, A. A. Some issues concerning devices and programs for automated learning. In A. A. Lumsdaine and R. Glaser (Eds.), *Teaching machines and programmed learning.* Washington: Natl. Education Assn., 1960. Pp. 517–539.

Lumsdaine, A. A. (Ed.) *Student response in programmed instruction.* Washington, D.C.: Nat'l Academy of Sciences—Nat'l Research Council, 1961.

Lumsdaine, A. A. Assessing the effectiveness of instructional programs. In R. Glaser (Ed.), *Teaching machines and programed learning, II: data and directions.* Washington: Natl. Education Assn., 1965.

Margulies, S. and L. D. Eigen. *Applied programed instruction.* New York: Wiley, 1962.

Melton, A. W. The science of learning and the technology of educational methods. *Harvard educ. Rev.,* 1959, **29**, 84–106.

Melton, A. W. *Categories of human learning.* New York: Academic Press, 1964.

Moore, O. K. Autotelic responsive environments and exceptional children. In *The special child in Century 21*. Seattle: Special Child Publications, 1964.

Ofiesh, G. D. and W. C. Meierhenry. (Eds.) *Trends in programmed instruction*. Washington: Natl. Educ. Assn., 1964.

Skinner, B. F. Teaching machines. *Scientific American*, 1961, **205** (5), 90–102.

Uttal, W. R. On conversational interaction. In J. E. Coulson (Ed.), *Programmed learning and computer-based instruction*. New York: Wiley, 1962. Pp. 171–190.

Date Due